Anonymous

Bancroft's Tourists Guide

Yosemite, San Francisco and Around the Bay

Anonymous

Bancroft's Tourists Guide
Yosemite, San Francisco and Around the Bay

ISBN/EAN: 9783744670609

Printed in Europe, USA, Canada, Australia, Japan

Cover: Foto ©Andreas Hilbeck / pixelio.de

More available books at **www.hansebooks.com**

BANCROFT'S

TOURIST'S GUIDE.

YOSEMITE.

SAN FRANCISCO AND AROUND THE BAY,
(SOUTH.)

SAN FRANCISCO:
A. L. BANCROFT & COMPANY,
1871.

PREFACE.

THIS is a Pocket Guide to Yosemite Valley and the Big Trees, with the best routes thither and thence. It also includes San Francisco with the cities, towns, caves, mines and beaches within a hundred miles south and east of this city.

We have tried to make it accurate and reliable in all statements of routes, distances, time required, conveyances, fares, hotels, rates, etc., making a snug, neat and tasteful book, to be sold at a low rate on all overland trains and ocean steamers bound hither, meeting all tourists, excursionists and travelers some hundreds of miles before they reach San Francisco, posting them on all the most attractive spots in the State, and answering in advance all necessary questions, thus enabling them, before setting foot in the city, to plan their excursions, decide upon routes, choose conveyances, select hotels, and calculate expenses. And then, when they have actually been over the whole ground, and thoroughly tested it, find everything *"just as the book said."*

True, we already have three or four costly volumes, written for a similar purpose, but we claim that for the ordinary use of the average tourist this is superior to any or all of them in at least three important particulars:

1st. It omits all tedious, long-drawn, and unnecessarily minute descriptions, which may occasionally suit some very critical or scientific tourist, but whose chief value is to *guide* the traveler's money into the publisher's pocket.

2d. It contains brief descriptions of all the most notable curiosities and wonders of the State. Its statements are drawn from the latest official scientific source, or taken from the personal observation and actual measurements of the writer, made expressly for this work.

3d. It is compact and economical of time, space and money, none of which the tourist usually cares to waste or lose or throw away.

The public have called for it, and we have done our best to respond, with the material, and in the time, at our command.

That it contains *no* mistakes we do not claim, but that it includes fewer than any similar book we confidently affirm. We have availed ourselves of every practicable source of reliable information up to date, June, 1871.

In a new and fast-growing State, like ours, where railroad companies sometimes lay nearly a league of track a day, it is simply impossible that any publication should remain perfectly accurate in every particular, even for twenty-four hours after its issue.

We pledge ourselves to disappoint no reasonable expectation, and shall thankfully receive and gratefully appreciate any correction or later information which any traveler, railroad, stage or saddle-train agent, or hotel manager, will kindly communicate.

In response to many calls, constantly repeated, and now pressingly urged, we offer this little Common-sense Hand-book Guide, which truthfully tells tourists just

WHERE TO GO ; HOW FAR IT IS ; HOW TO GET THERE ;

WHEN TO START ; WHOM TO STOP WITH ;

HOW LONG IT TAKES; AND, HOW MUCH IT ALL COSTS.

SAN FRANCISCO, CAL., Jun., 1871.

YOSEMITE.

You are going to Yosemite. Of course you are. What else did you come to California for? The idea of a man in his right mind, having the slightest love of beauty, grandeur and sublimity, coming to California and *not* going to Yosemite! Why, it's preposterous; it's incredible; it's impossible. We may as well dismiss the thought at once. Of *course* you go. So that's settled.

Now, *when* will you go? If you have means and are sure of time to see all the wonders and beauties which the State offers, then might you wisely and safely leave the best until the last; that is, reserve Yosemite for your final trip before you return. But, lest time or cash should fail, or sudden summons hasten your departure, it is wisest and safest to make sure of it at once while you may. It would never do to go back East, confront inquiring friends, and have to humbly confess that you *had* been to California, but had *not* seen Yosemite.

Then, *how* shall you go. If you are fresh and strong, with the nerve and muscle of a young and enthusiastic college pedestrian, you can do it on foot, as Bayard Taylor did Europe. It's the most independent and enjoyable way of all if you have time and disposition, and no ladies in your party. If you *should* wish to try that, get a copy of the Overland Monthly for July, 1870, turn to the article "Yosemite on Foot," and you have your guide.

If you haven't time or ambition to distinguish yourself by emulating Weston, you may possibly contemplate an excursion on hoofs. Several parties have done Yosemite on all fours, and report a tough American nag, or a wiry little Mexican mustang as an indispensable auxiliary. Parties who wish to avoid the sense of dependence, as well as the pecuniary expense of hiring a stable horse, frequently buy a tough native horse for seventy-five or a hundred dollars, use him for the entire trip, with no expense beyond that of daily feeding, keep him until they have finished their tour, and then sell him for nearly as much, in some cases even more, than they paid.

Mounted in this way you accomplish a sort of vicarious pedestrianism, gladly substituting equine hoofs for human heels, while the animal himself rejoices in a responsible backer in the bifurcated person of your bestriding self; or, still again, it may be—it probably *does* be, as our little four-year-old says—that you are too fashionably *lazy*,—I beg pardon, I meant to say, it is possible that you have inherited a constitutional aversion to protracted exertion, which, by long indulgence, has quite unfitted you for the thoroughly manly or womanly pursuit of grandeur, beauty, and pleasure in the saddle—chasing health on horseback.

One other way remains, before you fall back upon the fashionable and feeble way of "being carried" in the regular, orthodox and popular style, which suffers you to attempt no personal exercise beyond "the heavy looking on." You may combine saddle and wagon: that is, take a strong wagon, carrying tent, provisions and cooking apparatus, with one or two of the more unskillful riders on the seat, while the others in the saddle revolve as equestrian satellites around.

But if you decide, as most do, and as you probably will, to take no responsibility and cumber yourself with no care, you select one of the various public routes, seek out its agent, make your contract, give up all planning and providing on your own part, pay over your coin, take your tickets for the round trip, commit yourself to one of the various lines of public conveyances, dismiss all anxiety and give yourself up to receive and absorb all the pleasure that may lie along the route, or await you at its end.

And if your object is simply enjoyment, untroubled by exertion, and unmixed with anxiety, that is, undoubtedly, the best way.

You are in San Francisco, at the Grand, at the Occidental, at the Lick House or the Cosmopolitan. In their luxurious beds you have slept off the fatigue of thirty-three hundred miles across the continent, and at their bountiful tables you have fed yourself into courage and spirit for new and further enterprise. You have come forth so fresh and brave that you feel ready for eight thousand miles more, straight across the tranquil Pacific; or climbing, unaided, the loftiest vertebral peak of that spinal range which furnishes the backbone of the continent. Your new vigor has let off its frothy effervescence in sundry spasmodic dashes about the city and around its suburbs. You have driven to the Cliff House, interviewed the seals, climbed Telegraph hill, rusticated at Woodward's, spent an afternoon at Bancroft's, crossed to Oakland, inspected Alcatraz and Fort Point, and, in short, completed the little day-trips and half-day tours which so restfully entertain the newly-arrived traveler, gradually acclimate him to our occidental air and familiarize him with our cosmopolitan people. You feel strong and fresh: ready for the grand excursion. All your drawing-room and dining-table suits are snugly packed in trunks, folded away in drawers or carefully hung in wardrobe or clothespress. The roughest, strongest and warmest suit in your possession you have donned. Specially provide good stout, yet easy, boots or shoes, with the softest and most comfortable of socks or stockings. Remember that every day brings two climates, a cool or even cold one for morning and evening, with a hot and dusty noon sandwiched between. Umbrellas and rubber blankets you won't need, though a good traveling shawl will serve you frequently and well. Stovepipe hats are an abomination—a hard hat of any shape, first cousin to it, and the extra wide brimmed ladies' picnic hat, closely akin to both. Browns, drabs and grays are your best colors; linens and woolens your best materials; fine flannels next the skin, and especially provide plenty of something soft and thick to come between you and the horse, during the necessary miles in the saddle. This last is not a matter of choice, but of necessity. Calculate to spend at least two weeks in the valley, and allow two or even three days each way for your trip in and out. Of course you can go faster and quicker if you wish or must, but of all excursions imaginable, Yosemite most needs deliberation and leisure. These are precisely the two things of which the average American tourist has the least. Whence it has happened that very few indeed, especially of our own countrymen, have ever really *visited* Yosemite. Hundreds have dashed in, plunged around and rushed out. Horace Greeley staid about as long as it would take him to rush off one of his patent chain-lightning, hieroglyphic Tribune editorials.

He rode in at midnight, reached his lodging at one o'clock in the morning, too tired to eat, and too sore to tell of it; went to bed, sick, sore and disgusted. Up late next morning, so lame he could hardly sit in his saddle, hobbled hurriedly around three or four hours, and was on his way out again at a little after noon.

Many of the grandest sights he didn't even catch the remotest glimpse of; those he did see he just glanced at, too weary to appreciate their slightest beauty, and too hurried to allow himself time to begin to grow to the true scale of their grandeur; and having given to the whole valley about one quarter of the time necessary to thoroughly study, intelligently enjoy and yeartily appreciate the least of its wonders, he has the presumption to fancy he has "been to Yosemite." The fact is, he never really *saw* a single object about the valley, except, possibly, the giant cliff, Tu-toch-ah-nu-lah, which, as he says, looked as if it might have leaned over and buried him beneath its vastness, and which, as I say, *would*, doubtless, have done so speedily, had it known that the shabby rider who shambled along under its base that moonlight night, sore at one end, sleepy at the other, and sick all the way between, was going to rush off and talk so inadequately, unworthily and even untruthfully about objects which no human eye ever did see or could see in the condition of his sleep-oppressed optics on that slumbrous August morning. He has the cheek to declare that the fall of Yosemite is a humbug. It would be interesting to know what the fall thought of Greeley. One thing is sure, all earlier and later visitors unite in the opinion that the only humbug in the valley that year went out of it in his saddle about three o'clock on that drowsy August afternoon, and has never since marred the measureless realities which he sleepily slandered. The simple fact is, Mr. Greeley saw the little which he did see three or four months too late in the season. If he ever comes again, at the right time, and stays to really *see* the wonders of the valley, he will be heartily ashamed of what he then wrote, and freely pardon his present critic. Meantime, exit H. G. We bear thee no malice. The soul that can see and feel as little as thine did in Yosemite provokes no anger, but only sorrow and compassion. For the sake of thy sore and raw and sadly-pummeled body, we freely forgive the terribly shaken soul that inhabited it on that memorable midnight when horse and saddle maliciously united in assault and battery on the most sensitive portion of thine editorial corporosity. Vale, Greeley, vale. The next time thou comest hither, wear what hat thou likest and match it with what suit may please thee best, but if thou lovest life, and wouldst see good days, tell, oh Horace, tell the truth.

Pardon our digression to Greeley. We have spent so much time on him, not because he occasionally scribbles illegible manuscript for a new and struggling paper in a small eastern village, but because he came faster, arrived sorer, stayed fewer hours, saw less of the valley, and slandered it more than any one else has ever attempted.

Olive Logan spoke disparagingly of the Yosemite Fall, but the Fall is still there. She adds some slanderous remarks about the conduct of the drivers along the route, to which the only fitting answer would be these questions: "When a man or a woman, all alone in a room, looks into a mirror, and doesn't see a gentleman or lady reflected therein—*whose fault is it?* Is the difficulty in the glass or in *front* of it?

But let us start. From San Francisco to Yosemite there are three routes. All of them carry one, first, to or near Stockton, which city we reach by rail or river, and all of them bring us, at last, into the valley by one of the only two trails which enter it. Between the outer ends of these trails and Stockton, or vicinity, lie the various intermediate places or way stations which have given name to the routes which pass through them, and concerning which the tourist chiefly needs reliable information.

Looking upon any good map, not drawn in the exclusive interest of some one of these rival routes, you can easily see for yourself, spite of all agents' representations, which is the most direct way, geographically or topographically.

We now mention these in regular order, reckoning from north to south; that is, *down the map,* as we used to say at school. For convenience, we may distinguish the three routes as the upper or north route, the middle route, and the lower or south route.

Big Oak Flat Route.

The upper or north route is commonly called the Big Oak Flat, or the Hutchings route. If we go by this, we can either go directly into the valley, or make a detour by way of the Calaveras Big Trees. The following table showing distances, times and conveyances, by the straight and quick way.

TO YOSEMITE VALLEY—DIRECT.

From	To	Miles.	Hours.	By
San Francisco	Stockton	90	10	Steamer.
Stockton	Milton	28	1¼	Car.
Milton	Chinese Camp	24	4	Stage.
Chinese Camp	Garrote	14	2½	"
Garrote	Tamarack	32	6	"
Tamarack	Yosemite	11	4	Saddle.
		199	27¾	

By the above way you leave San Francisco at four o'clock P.M., from the wharf, at the foot of Broadway, by one of the California Pacific Railroad Company's steamers for Stockton. You have a fine afternoon and sunset view of San Francisco, the shipping, Oakland, Yerba Buena and Alcatraz Islands, the Golden Gate, Angel Island, Mount Tamalpais, San Quentin, San Pablo Bay, Vallejo, Mare Island, Suisun Bay, Benicia, Martinez, and Mount Diablo. Those who have crossed the continent by rail find this sail a pleasant change. They avoid the dust, get a good night's rest on the steamer, reach Stockton at from two to three o'clock in the morning, breakfast at six, and at seven take the cars of the Stockton and Copperopolis Railroad from the station near the landing. We reach Milton, twenty-eight miles, at 8.20, find the stage waiting, and immediately embark, and are off at once. The road lies through a mountainous country, well timbered. The air is clear and invigorating, and the scenery sublime. The road is good, the stages first-class, and the drivers obliging.

About one we reach Chinese Camp, and after twenty-four miles staging are ready for a half-hour's rest and a good dinner; or, we may wait for both until we reach Garrote, fourteen miles farther. Here either of two good hotels will feed and lodge us. Next morning we'd better dress for the horse-back ride in the afternoon. Lay aside all superfluous luggage and pack your extra nice clothing, if you have been foolish enough to bring any, in your valise. A small hand-satchel you can pack behind you on the horse, or take it before you. Let it be as small and snugly-packed as possible. One word further, and a most important one, especially to ladies. Calculate to *ride astride*, and dress for it. You can wear a long skirt to Tamarack, but beyond it is a nuisance. A woman who has only one leg, or has two on one side, may have some excuse for the unnatural, ungraceful, dangerous and barbarous side-saddle. The last word was prompted by remembering the raw back of the beautiful horse which carried Miss Dix into the valley, under the old, conventional, side-saddle. The lady is, unquestionably, a noted philanthropist, but that poor horse probably never suspected it. Anna Dickinson rode in man-fashion, arrived fresh and strong, and so did her horse. Ask her animal if he wants to carry that lady again and he'll never say nay (neigh). On a trip like this the side-saddle is barbarous to the horse and dangerous to the rider. The only good thing about it is that it jolts and racks and strains and tires the rider so outrageously, that it is fast converting many women to the sensible and safe way.

From Tamarack Flat the road dwindles to a trail, winds among pine trees, crosses an occasional rivulet, commands a fine outlook through the trees, now and then, and finally, almost before you know it, brings you to the brink of the valley. Thence let your horse have his head. He'll take care of himself and you too—land you safely at the foot of the trail, and deposit you at Hutchings' by five or six o'clock, in good time for the ample dinner which will be waiting.

If you wish to take the Calaveras Big Trees on your way, you can do so, either going or coming, by taking the same general route as far as Milton, to which place the times, distances, and conveyances are the same as in the table already given. From Milton you take stage through Murphy's to Sperry & Perry's hotel, where you dine in the very shadows of the Big Tree grove. Having stayed among the vegetable monsters as long as you can, you return thence by stage to Sonora, twenty-nine miles; time six hours; from Sonora to Garrote, also by stage, twenty-five miles in five hours, and then you strike the same road which you would travel by going directly in, so that the conveyances, time and distances of the former table will also serve you hence. As we said a few paragraphs back, these two routes are not really separate and distinct routes, as nearly one hundred and twenty miles on the western end, and about fifty miles at the eastern end, are the same in both. The time occupied in going or coming by the way of the trees is twelve and one half hours more than by the direct route, and the fare is seven dollars more, besides, of course, the expense of one night's lodging and two meals more on the route, than will be necessary to one going directly in.

The second route, the middle one, is the

Coulterville Route,

so named from the principal town through which it passes, which took its own name from General Coulter, who still manages the business of the line.

By this route you leave San Francisco at four P. M, by cars on Central Pacific Railroad ; change cars at Lathrop for Modesto, arriving same evening. Remain over night at the Ross House, James Cole, proprietor, and leave by stage at eight A. M. for Coulterville, forty-eight miles, ten hours, arriving at six P. M.

You dine at La Grange, twenty-eight miles from Modesto. Stay all night at Wagner's Hotel, Coulterville, where supper, lodging and breakfast cost you $2.50.

Next morning rise early, take a good hot breakfast, leave Coulterville at five o'clock for Gobin's Ranch at Crane's Flat, thirty miles, where you are due at twelve. Dine at Gobin's for $1.00. At one o'clock leave Gobin's by saddle train, arriving at Black's Hotel, in the valley, fifteen miles, at six P. M., thus taking it leisurely, especially down the mountain-side trail into the valley, where no animal can go fast and keep his feet, and no rider can hurry and save his neck.

Returning, leave the valley at six in the morning, and reach Gobin's, Crane Flat, at eleven, taking five hours, the same time as when going in, as horses can go full as fast *up* the trail as down. Dine at Gobin's, as when going in. Leave Crane Flat at twelve, and reach Coulterville at half past five, where the same hotel, Wagner's, accommodates you with supper, lodging and breakfast, and at the same rates as before.

Leave Coulterville at six next morning, and drive twenty-eight miles to Roberts', where we dine, at noon. From Roberts' to

Modesto is twenty miles. We are due at Modesto at from four to half past four P. M. From Modesto we may take cars for Stockton and Sacramento, at five, and go through direct to either of those places. But if we wish to return to San Francisco, we stop at Lathrop, in a station where an excellent dinner or supper can be had for 75 or 50 cents; and wait until eleven p. m., when a freight train, with sleeping car attached, comes along, and bring us to San Francisco at half past seven next morning.

This route gives regular rest, takes one through a beautiful and picturesque country, from the fact that, after striking the foot-hills, it lies along the dividing ridge between the Tuolumne and Merced rivers. On the east lies the Sierra Nevada, with Castle Peak, Mount Dana, and other prominent points, while westward it commands a view of the San Joaquin Valley and the Coast Range. To this may be added the fact that as a good part of the road runs east and west, and as the prevailing winds are northerly, the dust is blown away to one side instead of along with you.

Another and very great advantage of this route is that, from and after the fifteenth of this month, June, 1871, it will run stages to the very brink of the valley, leaving but two and a half miles of saddle riding to the valley below, and only seven miles on horseback to the hotels. This same advantage will then be true, also, of the Big Oak Flat, or Hutchings' route, which enters the valley by the same trail.

Mariposa Route.

This is the lower, or southern route, taking its name from that of its chief town, Mariposa, once famous as the seat of Fremont's famous "estate," with its gold mines of supposed exhaustless wealth.

This route takes one by California Pacific Railroad from San Francisco, through Lathrop to Modesto, one hundred and one miles; thence ninety-six miles of staging, through

Snelling's, Hornitos, Bear Valley, and White & Hatch's (stop over night) to Clark & Moore's, at the end of staging. From Clark's to the brink of the valley, by saddle, is twenty-three miles, and thence to the hotels, seven miles; making a total of thirty miles horseback riding. As an offset to this the Mariposa Route claims the advantage of the view from Inspiration Point, which lies nearly a mile off the direct trail, and for grandeur and beauty is certainly all that can be claimed or desired.

Besides the view from Inspiration Point, this route also presents the attraction of the Mariposa Big Trees, six miles from Clark's, and requiring an additional expense of $2.50 for each horse, besides the cost of another day's board and the fee of the guide.

The Calaveras trees, while equally grand and beautiful and even loftier, have the great advantage of an excellent hotel in the very midst of them, so that the tourist can spend much more time in rambling among their monumental bulks.

Besides the three routes already named, two others have been opened during the present season. The first of these may be called the

Mokelumne Hill Route.

Parties of eight, leaving San Francisco on the morning train, or Sacramento on the noon train, can take stage at Mokelumne station, at 1.30 P. M., reach Mokelumne Hill the same evening at seven o'clock, stay all night, and reach the Calaveras Big Trees at noon next day.

Price, from San Francisco to the Trees, and return, $17.00; from Sacramento to the Trees and back, $15.50. Parties of four will be taken for $15.00 each from Mokelumne station to the trees and back, in first class coaches and carriages. Any wishing to try this route can address Peck & Co., Mokelumne Hill.

From the trees one can go on to the valley by regular stages, and come out by any trail he likes, by making previous arrangements accordingly.

The second additional route is known as

Hamilton's New Route.

By this route the tourist from either San Francisco or Stockton takes the Western Pacific Railroad to Galt, whence stages leaving at one P. M., carry him by the way of Ione City and Valley, through Jackson to Mokelumne Hill, where he arrives at 7 P.M., and stays over night.

Leave Mokelumne Hill at 6.30 next morning; take the direct route through Railroad Flat and reach the Big Trees at noon. Fare, for the round trip from San Francisco or Sacramento, $20,00. From either city to the Big Trees, $12.00, leaving one free to go from the grove to Yosemite, when and as he likes.

Independent Trips,

Are commonly made in one of three ways:

1st. By private wagons, taking camping apparatus, cooking utensils and provisions along.

2d. In the saddle, taking apparatus, utensils and food along on pack horses.

3d. On foot, taking as little as possible, and depending mainly on hotels and wayside ranches or farm houses for the necessary meals and lodging, unless you choose to lodge in your own blankets.

I. BY PRIVATE WAGONS.

Parties of from four to thirty try this method every season, and report themselves delighted with the enjoyment of it, and subjected to an average expense not exceeding $2.00 a day for each one of a party less than eight, or $1.50, or even less, a day for a party of from twelve to thirty.

II. BY SADDLE AND PACK ANIMALS.

By this method the party is still more independent than by wagons, as hoofs can go where wheels cannot. The expense is about the same, as what is saved in the hire of wagons is balanced by the cost of the greater number of horses where there must be one animal for each person in the party, besides from one to four, or even six, animals to carry camp equipage and food.

III. ON FOOT.

For complete independence, combined with the ability to go where and as you please, unconfined by roads or trails, this is the best way of all. You can feed and lodge at hotels and wayside houses, or you can take along blankets and lodge where night overtakes you. To the untrained this may seem exceedingly rough and uncomfortable; to those who have fairly tried it, you will have no need to recommend it.

Hotel Rates along these Routes.

The hotel rates vary but little by whatever route you may go or come. You will seldom find a meal or a lodging as low as fifty cents, especially among the mountains and at the places most frequented by summer travel. The more common price is seventy-five cents for either, and as we approach the Valley, or the Big Trees, we may calculate on that figure as the usual cost. The reasonable tourist,—and those who have souls great enough to lead them to nature's wonders are supposed to be reasonable at least,—will readily see two good reasons why the charges along routes like these must be relatively higher than along the more frequently and permanently traveled routes of the thickly settled portions of the State: 1st, Everything which requires transportation, furniture, carpets, and all articles of food which cannot be raised in the immediate vicinity, necessarily cost much more for transporttation than where steamers or cars bring them almost to the door. 2nd, The travel along all such routes, and the consequent profit upon that travel, must be made within less than one third of the year. During the remaining two thirds, furniture must stand unused, and nearly the whole amount invested for the accommodation of tourists must remain idle, not only yielding no income, but actually becoming a source of additional expense until the opening of a new season.

We have no disposition to apologize for any extortionate or unreasonable charges; for we are very happy to say that any such apology is rarely needed. Every experienced and fair-minded traveler knows that his fellow passengers are unreasonable and extortionate in *their* demands fully as often as the transportation companies and their agents are in theirs. The various lines into the Valley and the Big Trees are managed by men who realize perfectly well that the amount of patronage they receive, and consequently, the profits which they make, must depend upon their gaining and keeping the good will of the traveling public. There is plenty of opposition; among the rival lines, no one has or can obtain any monopoly.

The sensible and safe way, here, as everywhere, is to make a definite agreement beforehand. Don't trust *any* stranger's assurance that "we'll make *that all right.*" That very fair sounding phrase has made more trouble than almost any other of equal length. The trouble is that it has two meanings. The speaker's "all right" means, for himself, and the hearer's "all right" means for *himself*, too; hence the frequent upshot of such loose understanding is, that it proves a complete *mis*understanding, when they come to settle. Distinctly specify what is to be done; how it is to be done; by whom and when; and then add at least ten per cent. to the specified cost for those little extras which will inevitably force themselves upon you in almost every trip. Thus you may escape adding yourself to the list of those improvident ones whose usual exclamation at the close of any pleasure trip is "It cost me a great deal more than I *expected; and I always thought it would.*"

Valley Hotels.

There are three—Hutching's, Black's, and Liedig's. Any of them will keep you well for from $3.00 to $3.50 a day, or $20.00 a week. Hutchings' is the farthest up the valley and nearer the greater number of points of interest. Hutchings himself, as poor Dan Setchell used to make Captain Cuttle say of his friend "Ole Sol Gills," is the "chuck-fulledest man o' science," in all matters pertaining to the valley and its history, that one can find in the State. He keeps an excellent house and usually entertains the more distinguished literary and scientific tourists. The Yosemite branch of the Western Union Telegraph now completed and working as far as Garrote, will be extended into the valley and have its office at Hutchings, by July 1st.

Black's is a new house, built expressly for the increased travel of late years—having excellent bath and other accommodations, with well-finished and furnished rooms. It stands three quarters of a mile nearer the west end of the valley.

Liedig's is also new, and is specially noted for the bountiful supply of well-cooked food which usually loads its hospitable table, under the immediate and personal superintendence of its obliging hostess. It is situated nearly in front of the base of Sentinel Rock.

Each of these houses, of course, has its warm friends, loud in its praises. All of them do their best for the satisfaction of guests and any one of them will provide the tourist with a comfortable home.

Horses and Guides in the Valley.

For a good horse and saddle the charge is $2.50 a day, or for a trip, if it occupies such part of the day that the animal cannot go out on any other one the same day. If you propose to stay a week or more, and wish to engage the same horse for your regular and exclusive use every day during that time, you can do so for one fifth less; sometimes lower than that.

The horses are good, trusty, serviceable beasts, trained to their business and generally safe and reliable.

Going into or coming out from the valley with any regular trip, over any route, you have nothing to do with providing or paying for a guide. One accompanies the saddle-train each way.

In and about the valley, you can have the company and attention of a practiced and competent guide for $3.00 a day—or, a trip. The guide's fee is the same whether the party be small or large.

No tourist who has the nerve and muscle of an average man or woman really *needs* either horse or guide. The valley is only seven miles long and but a mile wide. The perpendicular walls, from three to five thousand feet high, shut you in all around. You certainly can't get *out;* and with so many prominent landmarks all about you, you can't get *lost*, unless you try very hard indeed. With a good guide-book before you and well-rested legs under you, a very moderate exercise of common sense will take you all about the valley, and enable you thoroughly to explore its wonders "on foot and alone" if you choose so to go.

Bear in mind, however, that you are nearly a mile—in some places more than a mile—above the sea; that the atmosphere is rare and light; that you need to restrain your impulse to *dash* about, especially at first. For the first two or three days "go slow"—take it moderately; see *less* than you think you might, rather than more. As you become more familiar with the character of the rocks and ravines and accustomed to the exertion of climbing about them, you can extend your excursions and attempt harder things.

For the longer trips, such as the ascent of the Sentinel Rock, it may be safer and wiser to employ a good guide.

Expenses,

The total necessary expenses by each route are:

1st. By Big Oak Flat (Hutchings') Route:

From San Francisco to Yosemite Valley, *or* return.........	$20
From San Francisco to Yosemite *and* return	38
From San Francisco to the Calaveras Big Trees, *or* return.	10
From San Francisco to the Calaveras Big Trees and Valley, *or* return.................................	25
From San Francisco to the Calaveras Big Trees and Valley, *and* return.................................	45

Thomas Houseworth & Co., Agents, 317 and 319 Montgomery street, San Francisco.

2d. By the Coulterville Route:

From San Francisco to Yosemite Valley, *or* return.........	$20
From San Francisco to Yosemite Valley, *and* return........	38

G. W. Coulter, Agent, 214 Montgomery street, San Francisco.

3d. By Mariposa Route:

From San Francisco to Yosemite Valley, *or* return.........	$25
From San Francisco to Yosemite Valley, *and* return........	45

Ed. Harrison, Agent, Grand Hotel, San Francisco.

Board and Lodging en route, per day.................	$3 00
Board and Lodging in the Valley, per day..............	3 00
Board and Lodging at Big Trees, per day	3 00
Board and Lodging in either place, per week...........	20 00
Horses in Valley, or to Big Trees, per day.............	2 50
Guides in Valley or to Big Trees, per day	3 00

TOTAL EXPENSES OF EXCURSION.

1. To Yosemite Valley, direct, by Big Oak or Coulterville, stay one week in the Valley, hiring guide and horse three days, and returning by same route...................... $80

2. Above excursion, including Calaveras Big Trees...... 90
3. To Yosemite Valley direct, by Mariposa, staying a week in the Valley, hiring guide and horse three days, and coming out same way.. 87
4. Above excursion, including Mariposa Big Trees...... 93
5. In by Big Oak Flat or Coulterville, and out by Mariposa, or *vice versa*, other conditions as above............... 87
6. In by Mariposa, and out by Big Oak Flat, visiting *both* groves of Big Trees, same conditions as above............. 110

In the above statement the expense for guide is based on the supposition that the party includes at least three persons.

YOSEMITE VALLEY.

THE name is Indian. Pronounce it in four syllables, accenting the second. It means "Big Grizzly Bear."

The valley lies very near the centre of the State, reckoning north and south, about one fifth the way across from east to west, and almost exactly in the middle of the high Sierras which inclose it. Its direction from San Francisco is a little south of east, and its distance about one hundred and forty miles in an air line. The valley itself lies nearly east and west. Its main axis runs a little north of east by a little south of west.

It consists of three parts:

1st. The surrounding wall of solid rock, nearly vertical, and varying in height from one thousand to four and even five thousand feet.

2d. The slope of rocky masses and fragments which have fallen from the face of the cliffs, forming a sort of *talus* or escarpment along the foot of this wall, from seventy-five to three hundred and fifty feet high, throughout the greater part of its extent.

3d. The nearly level bottom land, lying between these slopes, forming the valley proper, and divided into two unequal parts by the Merced River flowing through westerly, from end to end.

The main valley is seven miles long; though one may make it longer if he estimates the branches or divisions at the upper or eastern end. Its width varies from a few feet on either side of the stream, to a full mile and a quarter in its broadest part. It contains over a thousand acres; two thirds meadow, and the rest a few feet higher, somewhat sandy, gravelly, and, in places, covered with rocks and boulders from the surrounding cliffs. Over the latter portion, at irregular intervals, trees, shrubs and ferns are sparsely sprinkled or set in irregular groups. The richer bottom supports several fine clumps and groves of graceful trees.

The bottom of the valley is four thousand feet above the level of the sea, and has an average fall, towards the west, of about six feet to the mile. The river varies in width from fifty to seventy feet, and in depth from six to twelve feet. Its bottom is gravelly, its current remarkably swift, its waters clear as crystal. Trout, of delicious quality, abound, but seldom allow white men to catch them.

The rocky wall which shuts it in, averages over three quarters of a mile in perpendicular height. Nothing on wheels has ever gone up or down this tremendous precipice, and in only two places have the surest-footed horses or mules been able to find a safe trail.

Yosemite Valley is really a huge sink or cleft in a tangle of rock-mountains; a gigantic trough, not scooped or hollowed out from above, but sunk straight down, as if the bottom had dropped plumb toward the centre, leaving both walls so high that if either should fall, its top would reach clear across the valley and crash against the opposite cliff several hundred feet above its base.

In many places these cliffs rise into rock-mountains, or swell into huge mountainous domes, two or three of which have been split squarely in two, or cleft straight down from top to bottom, and the two halves, still standing straight up, have been heaved or thrown a half-mile asunder, whence each looks wistfully across at its old mate, or frowns sternly and gloomily down upon the beautiful valley which quietly keeps them apart.

Here and there they tower into lofty spires, shoot up in shattered or splintered needles, or solemnly stand in stately groups of massive turrets. High bastions surmount steep precipices, and both look down on awful chasms.

Back from the edge of the valley, behind these cliffs, the rock country stretches away in every direction through leagues of solid granite, rising irregularly into scattered hills, peaks and mountains, between which run the various snow-fed streams, whose final, sudden plunge over the valley's sharp and rocky brink makes the numerous falls of such wonderful height.

. Coming in by either trail, one enters the western or lower end of the valley. We will suppose ourselves entering by the Mariposa trail. We have clambered, or allowed our animals to clamber, safely down the rocky, steep, and crooked trail, which lands us finally at the foot of the precipitous slope of two thousand seven hundred feet. As we follow the trail up the valley, that is, bearing away to the right, going eastward along the foot of the south wall, we encounter the falls, mountains, spires and domes in the following order:

One coming in by the Coulterville, Hardin's or Big Oak Flat trail, finds himself at the same end of the valley, directly opposite the foot of the Mariposa trail, having the river between; and as he bears away to the left, along the base of the north wall, he would, of course, meet all these wonders in exactly the reverse order. But to return to the foot of the Mariposa or Clark's trail:

First, the

Bridal Veil Fall,

Indian name Po-ho-no, meaning, " The Spirit of the Evil Wind." The fall is over nine hundred feet high, and of indescribable beauty. The stream which forms it has an average width of some sixty-five feet at the edge of the cliff where it breaks over the brink. It is narrower in summer and wider in winter. For six hundred and thirty feet the stream leaps clear of the cliff in one unbroken fall. Thence it rushes down the steep slope of broken rocks in a confusion of intermingled cascades nearly three hundred feet more.

The varying pressure of the changeful wind causes a veil-like waving, swaying and fluttering, which readily suggests the obviously fitting and most appropriate name.

> What could a bride be made of,
>   Who would wear a veil like this?
> No sooner asked than answered,
>   She must be "Maid o' the Mist."

This fall presents its greatest beauty in May or June when the volume of water is not too great. The situation of Pohono, added to its intrinsic beauty, waving a welcome as the tourist enters and fluttering a farewell as he leaves, make it the universal favorite. Ladies especially love to linger at its foot, feasting their eyes with its marvelous and changeful beauty, and delighting their hearts with the delicious suggestiveness of its most appropriate name. The honeymoon can nowhere be more fittingly or happily spent than within sight of Pohono.

Half a mile further the cliff rounds outward and

swells upward into an enormous double, rocky bastion, the

Cathedral Rocks.

Two thousand six hundred and sixty feet above the valley. Indian name, Po-see-nah Choock-kah, meaning a large store or hoard of acorns. From certain points of sight the form of these rocks readily suggests the outline of a dilapidated Gothic cathedral. Only the superior grandeur of Tutoch-ah-nu-lah and the South Dome, prevent this rock from greater fame. Outside of Yosemite it would quickly attain a world-wide celebrity.

Just beyond these rocks the cliff bears away to the southeast and sends up two slender, graceful pinnacles of splintered granite, rising five hundred feet above the main wall, which supports them. These are the

Cathedral Spires.

Their summits are twenty-four hundred feet above the valley. Seen from the northeast, a mile distant, these spires appear symmetrical, of equal height, squarely hewn and rising above the edge of the cliff behind, exactly like two towers of a Gothic cathedral. One who doubts the appropriateness of their name, has only to view them from this point, whence a single glance will end his skepticism. Beyond the spires the wall runs southeasterly a quarter of a mile, then curves through an easterly and northerly sweep into a north and south line. The whole sweep forms a sort of precipitous coast with its rocky headlands, inclosing the valley between like an emerald bay. Beyond this bay the rocky wall gradually curves again, and resumes its easterly trend. An eighth of a mile further brings us to

The Fissure.

This is a cleft or split in the rock, running back southeasterly at nearly a right angle with the face of the cliff. It is one thousand feet deep, five feet wide at the top and front, and grows gradually narrower as it extends downward and backward into the mountain. Several boulders have fallen into it and lodged at different depths.

A third of a mile east of this fissure, and a mile and three quarters from the Cathedral Rocks, another rocky promontory projects northwesterly, like a huge buttress, a third of a mile into the valley, crowned with a lofty granite obelisk, three hundred feet thick, and standing straight up twelve hundred feet above the giant cliff which supports it. This is the famous

Sentinel Rock.

so named from its resemblance to a gigantic watch-tower or signal station, for which, the legends say, the Indians formerly used it. The Indian name was Loya. Its top is three thousand and forty-three feet above the river at its foot. The sides show plainly-marked perpendicular cleavages in the granite.

Although so steep in front and at the sides, a strong grasp, a sure foot, a cool nerve and a calm head can safely climb it from the rear, that is, the southwest side. At least they have done so more than once, and planted a flag to wave in triumph from its summit. By the unanimous and unquestioned verdict of all tourists, this rock is one of the grandest and most beautiful even in Yosemite itself. Its striking prominence has made it a favorite subject with all artists who have visited the valley.

Three quarters of a mile southeast of the sentinel tower, half a mile back from the brink of the precipice, and partially or totally hidden by it, according as the spectator stands nearer to or farther from the foot of the cliff, the

Sentinel Dome

lifts its hemispherical bulk four thousand one hundred and fifty feet. This is one of the most regularly formed of all of the peculiar dome-like peaks about the valley. The Indian name was Loy-e-ma. A horseman can reach the very summit by a trail up the eastern slope, and enjoy a most extensive view as his reward. From this dome, the profile of the South Dome and strongly marked moraines of the Too-loo-le-wack Cañon appear to better advantage than from any other point.

A mile east of Sentinel Rock the face of the cliff becomes less precipitous, bends sharply around to the south, and thence back towards the southwest, forming an angular and sloping rocky bluff known as

Glacier Rock,

called by the Indians, Oo-woo-yoo-wah, which means, the "Great Rock of the Elk." The story has it that during one of the expeditions of troops into the valley, a party of soldiers, searching for Indians, undertook to climb this rock, and while, slowly and with great labor, working their way up its smooth and steep slope, the hunted red men suddenly appeared upon its summit, and began to roll large stones down upon them. These came thundering down with terrific niose and frightful speed. The pale faces turned and fled with headlong haste, but the destructive missiles smote several of them with instant death.

From the point of Glacier Rock one has a fine view of the valley. All the domes, with the Yosemite, Vernal and Nevada Falls are plainly visible thence.

For nearly a mile southeast of Glacier Rock the cliff becomes steeper and more precipitous, forming the western wall of a wild, rough cañon, stretching away southeasterly for nearly a mile. Over the cliff at the head of this cañon the south fork of the Merced plunges six hundred feet in the

Illilouette Fall.

This is also called the Too-loo-le-wack, or Too-lool-we-ack Fall. The meaning of either of these Indian names is not certainly given. Cunningham, one of the oldest and best guides of the valley, calls the cañon and the fall at the head of it, the El-lil-o-wit. The tourist who attempts this cañon must leave all hoofs behind, and, falling back to first principles, depend entirely upon his own understanding.

Among the enormous masses of rock which obstruct it, several extensive fissures and romantic caverns furnish additional stimulus to the wonder-loving pedestrian. As General Coulter says: "rough is no name for it." It is one of the wildest places imaginable. Few tourists accomplish it, but those who do are amply repaid.

From the foot of the Il-lil-ou-ette Cañon make your way directly east, clamber along half a mile, or let your horse do it for you, then bear away to the right, slightly south of east, and you find yourself entering the cañon of the main Merced itself. Now pick your way carefully along, and, as soon as you feel sufficiently sure of your foothold, look about you, and look ahead. Did you ever see finer boulder-scenery in your life? Stop under the sheltering lee of this huge, church-like boulder, and don the oiled or rubber suit which awaits your hire. You can get on without it, but the spray will quickly wet you into a

"Dem'd damp, moist and disagreeable body,"

if you try it.

Now take a stout stick, a deep breath, hold firmly on to both and plunge sturdily along the ascending trail. The deepest, richest and greenest of moss lines the narrow foot-path on either hand. Look quickly; enjoy it while you may, for presently you find breath and sight nearly taken away together by heavy spray-gusts, rushing, wind-driven, down the cañon. Catching the intervals between, and catching your breath at the same time, you lift your nearly blinded eyes to the

Vernal Fall

four hundred and fifty feet high, one hundred feet wide, and from three to five feet deep where it breaks over the square-cut edge of the solid granite beneath. The name Vernal was given it on account of the greenness of its water as it plunges over the brink, as well as to distinguish it from the very white fall a mile above. The Indian name was Pi-wy-ack, which is differently translated to mean "a shower of crystals," or "the cataract of diamonds."

This fall pours in one solid unbroken sheet of emerald green, flecked and fringed with creamy foam, and filling the whole cañon below with a thick, and fine and ceaseless spray, which keeps its moss, and grass and foliage of a rich, deep green nowhere surpassed in nature. This spray also combines with the sunshine to develop another and a marvelous beauty. At almost any point along the trail for several rods below the fall, the visitor who is climbing in the morning has only to turn square about to find himself glorified by an exquisitely beautiful circular rainbow surrounding his head like a halo. This rainbow forms a complete circle of so small a diameter that the tourist who views it for the first time involuntarily stretches out his hands to grasp it.

The path is wet and slippery, and the ladder-stairs which carry one up the right-hand face of the cliff, just at the south edge of the fall, are steep and tiresome. But good oil or rubber suits keep out the wet, a good restful pause now and then keeps in the breath, while careful stepping and firm holding on rob the steepness and slipperiness of all their real danger. Scores of ladies go up and come down every season without accident or harmful fatigue.

Arrived at the top of the singularly square-cut granite cliff, we turn to the left, walk to the very edge of the stream and the brink of the fall, and gaze into the misty chasm in which the foot of the fall disappears. One need not fear to do so, for nature, as if with special forethought for the gratification of future guests, has provided a remarkable parapet of solid granite running along the very edge of the brink for several yards south of the fall, just breast high, and looking as if made on purpose for timid tourists to lean over, and gaze with fearless safety into the seething chasm in whose foaming depths the foot of the cataract shrouds itself in impenetrable mist.

This ceaseless mistiness makes it almost impossible to estimate or calculate the exact height of the fall with any satisfactory accuracy. Another variable element which enters into all conjectures of its height is the fact that the rock on which it strikes slopes sharply down for upwards of a hundred and sixty feet. Hence in late spring or early summer, when the volume and velocity of the river are greatest, the water, shooting further out, falls at the very base of this slope, and gives the fall a height of four hundred and seventy-five or even five hundred feet in May or June. In October, on the other hand, when the stream is at its lowest, the water, falling straight down, strikes upon the top of this slope, a hundred and sixty or seventy-five feet above its base, and thus diminishes the height of the fall by just that amount.

In its volume, this fall resembles Niagara more than any other in the valley. In width, of course, it falls far below, but its height is more than three times as great. It also resembles Niagara in its greatening on the gaze with each successive visit. In its approaches, in its surroundings, and in itself, the Vernal fall surpasses expectation and fully satisfies desire.

Half a mile above the Vernal is a small but beautiful gem of a little fall, called the

Kachoomah,

or Wild Cat Fall. The reason of the name is obvious to one standing a hundred feet below, and noting how the impetuous stream, breaking over the sharp edge of a huge transverse boulder, dashes against the sloping side of another; lying angularly across; and is thrown, or seems to spring, diagonally across towards the northern bank, readily, though roughly, suggesting the sudden side-spring of the animal for whom the observing red man named it.

Another half mile, and the rocky walls close together, shut us in and bar our further progress. The cañon narrows to a point, over whose right hand wall, close to the very angle of meeting, the same river, the main Merced, plunges its whole volume in the famous

Nevada Fall,

seven hundred feet high, seventy-five feet wide at the brink, and one hundred and thirty below. This fall is, in all respects, one of the grandest in the world. In height, in width, in purity and volume of water during the early summer, in graceful peculiarities and in grandeur of surrounding scenery, it is simply stupendous. Other falls, though few, surpass it in the single element of height, but in surrounding grandeur, in the harmony of beauty and magnificence, none equal this. None brings the visitor oftener to its foot, detains him with greater delight, or sends him away with more profound satisfaction.

The exact statement of the height of this fall is hindered by causes similar to those at the Vernal, viz: the constant and blinding spray around the bottom, and the consequent uncertainty as to the exact spot where the water strikes.

The rock beneath this fall is not vertical, but rather steeply inclined, having a slope of about eighty-five degrees through its upper half and not far from seventy-five degrees through its lower. Hence in summer, when tourists usually see it, the diminished force of the current causes the water rather to slide down the slope, than to shoot out over and fall clear of it, as in the spring. Thus, from June to November the Nevada is more properly a chute or slide than a fall. During this season the friction of the rock breaks the stream into a white froth; hence the name, Nevada, or Snowy Fall.

When the water is very low, the fittest thing to

which one could liken it would be to myriads of white lace or gauze veils hung over the face of the cliff, waving and fluttering in the wind. A party of ladies originated this figure, and it occurred also to Mr. Bowles in his fine descriptions of Yosemite wonders.

As one stands in the cañon below gazing at the Nevada, the Snowy Fall, away upon his left, about a third of a mile back from the brink of the northeast wall of the cañon, rises

Mt. Broderick,

or the Cap of Liberty, whose general outline suggests its name. Its rounded summit lifts its smooth, weather-polished granite two thousand feet above the fall and nearly five thousand above the main valley. It bears upon its crown a single juniper of enormous diameter.

Away to the right of the cañon, just peeping above the edge of the cliff, and nearly two miles south-southeast of the Nevada Fall, rises the steep, conical summit of the South Dome, or

Mt. Starr King,

reaching an estimated height of one mile above the valley. Next to the wonderful half-dome, this is the steepest and smoothest cone in the region. Indian name, See-wah-lam, meaning not known. Its exact height, like that of its great namesake, has never been satisfactorily settled.

Clambering back down this cañon, depositing our oiled or rubber suits, and experiencing an immediate sense of relief and lightness, we retrace the trail up which we came, bear away to the right, that is, going nearly northwest, proceed nearly or quite a mile round the base of a lofty buttress, and open the

Tenaya Cañon,

stretching away northeast nearly in a continuous line with the main valley itself.

About one mile up this cañon towers Yosemite's sheerest and loftiest isolated cliff, the

Half-Dome

itself. It is a bare crest of naked granite, four thousand seven hundred and forty feet high, cleft straight down in one vast vertical front on the Tenaya, or northwest side, while on the back, that is, toward the southeast, it swells off and rounds away with a dome-like sweep that utterly dwarfs the grandeur of a thousand St. Peters in one.

Following still on up the Tenaya Cañon, nearly two miles beyond the dome, and a thousand feet higher, rises the

Clouds' Rest,

a granite ridge, long, bare and steep, having its axis parallel with that of the valley, and falling away along its southeastern slope into the rocky mountain wilderness of the High Sierras. This is one of the few points about the valley which the Geological Survey has not yet measured. They estimated its height one thousand feet above that of the Half Dome, which would make its summit ten thousand feet, or nearly two miles above the sea level.

Beyond this, little of note invites the traveler's delay, so we make our way northwesterly straight across this cañon from the base of its southeasterly wall toward that of the opposite cliff. On the way, however,

Mirror Lake

arrests and enchants us. Surely water reflections were never more perfect. The Indian name Ke-ko-too-yem, Sleeping Water, was never more happily bestowed. Imagine a perfect water mirror nearly eight acres in extent, and of a temperament so calm and deep and philosophic that it devotes its whole life to the profoundest reflection. A mile of solid cliff above, a mile of seeming solid cliff beneath; for though the mind knows the lower to be only an image, the eye cannot, by simple sight alone, determine which is the solid original and which the shadowy reflection.

> Twin mountains, base to base, here meet the astonished eye;
> One towers toward heaven in substance vast,

> One looms below in shadow cast,
> As grand, as perfect as its peer on high.

In early morning, when no breeze ripples the lake, its reflections are, indeed, marvelously life-like. So exactly is every line and point repeated that the photographic view has puzzled hundreds to tell which mountain is in the air and which is in the water. The spectator who takes the photogram in his hand for the first time often hesitates for several minutes before he can determine which side up the picture should be held. The depth of the lake is from eight to twenty feet.

One sufficiently vigorous and persevering may push on up the Tenaya creek till he finds the

Tenaya Lake,

over a mile long, snugly nestled in among the mountains. This lies beyond the usual limit of tourists' excursions, but well repays a visit.

Nearly a mile northwest of the lake, and about a third of a mile back from the edge of the cliff, the

North Dome

lifts its rounded granite bulk three thousand five hundred and seventy feet above the valley. It looks as if built of huge, concentric, overlapping, hemispherical domes, piled one upon another, and having their overlapping edges irregularly broken away. On the valley side, that is, toward the south and southeast, it is so steep that no human foot has ever climbed it. In the rear, however, that is, toward the north and west, it falls away in a vast ridge or spine, along which one can easily gain the very summit of the dome itself. The Indian name was To-coy-ah, meaning the shade of an Indian baby basket.

Passing three quarters of a mile still down, we reach the angle or turn between the Tenaya cañon and the valley proper. In this turn, in fact forming the angle, stands the

Washington Column,

a rounded, columnar rock tower, partially standing forth from the abutting cliff behind. This reaches the height of two thousand five hundred feet.

Immediately beyond this large masses of the huge concentric, overlapping plates, have cracked off, slipped away and fallen, leaving rough bas-relief arches several hundred yards long, and projecting some scores of feet, like rudely-drawn gigantic eyebrows. These are commonly called the

Royal Arches,

or the Arched Rocks, but the Indian name, Hun-to, "The Watching Eye," will better satisfy the poetical visitor, unless, indeed, his Masonic proclivities quite overpower his poetic appreciation, in which case he will undoubtedly prefer the former title.

For the next mile and a half northwest nothing of special wonder for Yosemite detains us.

The relief is fitting and needful, not only that we may recover in some degree from the continued effect of the marvels already past, but, more especially, that we may rally in preparation for the most stupendous wonder of them all, the great

Yosemite Fall

itself. Here language ceases and art quite fails. No words nor paintings, not even the photogram itself, can reproduce one tithe of the grandeur here enthroned. A cataract from heaven to earth, plunging from the clouds of the sky to bury itself among the trees of the forest. The loftiest waterfall yet known upon the face of the globe.

Don't mention figures yet, please. When a man is overwhelmed with the sublime, don't plunge him into statistics. By and by, when we have cooled down to a safe pitch, we may condescend to hear the calm calculator project his inexorable mathematics into the very face of nature's sublimity and triumphantly tell us just *how* great this surpassing wonder is. But after all his exactest calculations, his absolute measurements and his positive assurances, one *feels* how small the fraction of real greatness which figures can express or the intellect apprehend. A cataract half a mile high, setting its forehead against the stars and planting its feet at the base of the eternal hills. Gracefully swaying from side to side in rhythmical vibration, swelling into grandeur in earlier spring, and shrinking into beauty under the ardency of summer heat; towering far above all other cataracts, it calmly abides, the undisputed monarch of them all.

A half mile is no exaggeration, for the official measurement of the State Survey makes the height two thousand six hundred and forty-one (2,641) feet—a *full* half mile, and *one foot more*.

The fall is not in one unbroken, perpendicular sheet, but in three successive leaps. In the upper fall, the stream slides over a huge rounded lip or edge of polished granite, and falls one thousand five hundred and eighty-seven feet in one tremendous plunge. Here its whole volume thunders upon a broad shelf or recess, whence it rushes in a series of roughly-broken cascades down a broken slope of over seven hundred feet in linear measurement, but whose base is six hundred and twenty-six feet perpendicularly below its top. From the bottom of this broken slope it makes a final plunge of four hundred and twenty-eight feet in one clear fall, and then slides off contentedly into the restful shadows of the welcoming forests below.

Its width, like that of all snow-fed streams, varies greatly with the season. In March or April, when the tributary snows are melting most rapidly, and myriads of streamlets swell its volume, the stream is from seventy-five to a hundred feet wide, where it suddenly slips over the smoothly-rounded granite at its upper brink. During the same season it scatters or spreads to a width of from three to four hundred feet, when it breaks upon the rocky masses below.

In later spring, or earlier summer, it dwindles to less than a third of its greatest bulk; and its most intimate friend, the veteran Yosemite pioneer, Hutchings, tells us that he has seen it when it hardly seemed more than a silver thread winding down the face of the cliff. Under a full moon, the element of weirdness mingles with its graceful grandeur, shrouds it with mystery, and transports one into a soft and dreamy wonder-land, from which he cares not to return.

A mile further on our way back toward the western end, brings us under, or in front of, the triple rocky group, or three-peaked stone-mountain, whose name, the

Three Brothers,

readily suggests itself to one standing in the proper place below. They are three huge, bluntly conical, rocky peaks, fronting nearly south, slightly inclined toward the valley and descending in height as they approach it. To the rude Indian fancy they might well suggest the name *Porn-porn-pa-sue*—"Mountains playing leap-frog,"—with which they christened them.

The highest, which is the northernmost, the one furthest back from the valley, is three thousand eight hundred and thirty feet high. The summit of this rock is readily reached by a trail from the rear, and affords a superb view of the valley and its surroundings. Nearly all who have enjoyed it consider it the very best to be had.

Another mile-and-a-half and the rocky wonders of Yosemite fitly culminate and terminate in

Tu-toch-ah-nu-lah,

"The Great Chief of the Valley" more commonly, though very weakly, called "El Capitan," an ordinary Spanish word, meaning simply, "the Captain;" good enough for a ferry-boat or river steamer, but entirely beneath the dignity of this most magnificent rock on the face of the earth.

Tu-toch-ah-nulah is an immense granite cliff, projecting angularly into the valley, toward the southwest. It has two fronts, one facing nearly west, the other southeasterly, meeting in a sub-acute angle. These two fronts are over a mile long, and three thousand three hundred feet high, smooth, bare and vertical, and bounded above by a sharp edge, standing pressed against the sky, which its Atlas-like shoulder seems made to uphold.

The State Survey, with all its scientific coolness, could not help saying, "*El Capitan* imposes upon us by its stupendous bulk, which seems as if hewed from the mountains on purpose to stand as the type of eternal massiveness. It is doubtful, if anywhere in the world, there is presented so squarely cut, so lofty and so imposing a face of rock." Starr King declared, "A more majestic object than this rock, I never expect to see on this planet." Horace Greeley, who enjoyed the rare experience of entering the valley by night, and in moonlight too, thus pays tribute to the Great Chief :

"That first, full, deliberate gaze, up the opposite height! Can I ever forget it? The valley here, is scarcely half a mile wide, while its northern wall of mainly naked, perpendicular granite, is at least four thousand feet high, probably more. But the modicum of moonlight that fell into this awful gorge, gave to that precipice a vagueness of outline, an indefinite vastness, a ghostly and weird spirituality. Had the mountain spoken to me in an audible voice, or begun to lean over with the purpose of burying me, I should hardly have been surprised."

After Tutochahnulah, nothing on earth can seem very grand or overpowering, and with this the wonders of the valley fitly close.

We have, by no means, seen all the falls, nor even mentioned all the peaks, but the others are of little note in Yosemite, though, elsewhere, tourists might go a thousand miles to see the least of them. This valley is, beyond comparison, the most wonderful and beautiful of all earthly sights. No matter how incredulous one may be before entering, the Great Chief and his tremendous allies, soon crush him into the most humble and complete subjection. Do not expect, however, that your first view will stagger your skepticism. On the contrary, it may even confirm it. Upon our first view of Tutochahnulah, as we were walking into the valley, one bright July forenoon, we stopped a mile and a half from its foot, collected ourselves for a calm, cool, mathematical judgment and said with all confidence, "That rock isn't over fifteen hundred feet high. It *can't* be. Why, just look at that tree near its base. That tree, certainly, can't be more than a hundred and twenty-five feet high, and certainly, the cliff doesn't rise more than ten times its height above it." But, unfortunately, we had forgotten that never before had we seen the works of nature on as grand a scale. One's judgment has to change its base. He has to reconstruct it; to adopt a new unit. Comparison serves him little, for he has no adequate standard by which to measure, or with which to compare the rock-mountains before him. They are like nothing else. They are a law unto themselves, and one must learn the law, the *new* law, before he can begin to enter the secret of their greatness. Look at that tree. Elsewhere you would call it lofty. It measures a hundred and fifty feet, and yet, that wall of solid rock behind rises straight up to twenty times its height above it.

Look again; now, turn away; shut eyes and think. Forget all former standards and adopt the new. Slowly you begin to "even" yourself to the stupendous scale of the gigantic shapes around.

Even Niagara requires two or three days before one begins to fully realize or truly appreciate its greatness. How much more, then, Yosemite, compared with which Niagara is but a very little thing! Then, on the other hand, one must remember that after he has adjusted himself to the new and grander scale of Yosemite, upon coming out into the midst of ordinary hills and mountains, for several days they seem low and flat and small.

A single visit to Yosemite dwarfs all other natural wonders and spoils one for all places else. He who has seen it listens quietly to the most enthusiastic rhapsodies of the most widely traveled tourists, and simply answers, with a calm, superior smile, "Ah, that's all very well, but you should see *Yosemite*."

The Traveler's University—should such an institution ever exist—can never righteously graduate the most widely traveled tourist, until he can truthfully add to his name, "Y. S. T."—Yosemite Tourist.

THE BIG TREES.

Teh California Big Trees are a kind of Redwood; or, if the strictest and most scientific judgment does not rank them in the same family, it must, at least, allow a very close relationship.

Nine groves are already certainly known, and, every year or two, as the exploration of the State becomes more exact, or approaches completion, other smaller groves, straggling groups or solitary clumps, are added to the number. Of all those thus far discovered the Calaveras Grove and the Mariposa Grove are the most celebrated, both from the extent of the groves and the size and height of the trees composing them.

The Calaveras Grove

receives its name from that of the county in which it stands. It is near the source of the south fork of the Calaveras river, while the upper tributaries of the Mokelumne and the Stanislaus rivers flow near it: the former on the north, the latter on the southeast. It is about sixteen miles from Murphy's Camp, and on or near the road crossing the Sierras by the Silver Mountain Pass. This grove

THE CALAVERAS GROVE. 53

has received more visitors and attained greater celebrity than any other, for four reasons:

1st. It was the first discovered.

2d. It was nearer the principal routes of travel, hence more easily accessible.

3d. One can visit it on wheels.

4th. Last, and best for the tired tourist, an excellent hotel at the very margin of the grove; Sperry & Perry, proprietors.

The grove extends northeast and southwest about five eighths of a mile. Its width is only about one fifth as great. It stands in a shallow valley between two gentle slopes. Its height above the sea is four thousand seven hundred and fifty-nine feet. In late spring or early winter a small brook winds and bubbles through the grove; but under the glare of summer suns and the gaze of thronging visitors, it modestly "dries up."

The grove contains about ninety trees which can be called really "big," besides a considerable number of smaller ones deferentially grouped around the outskirts. Several of the larger ones have fallen since the grove was discovered, in the spring of 1852; one has had the bark stripped off to the height of one hundred and sixteen feet, and one has been cut down, or, rather, bored and sawed down. The bark thus removed was exhibited in different cities in this country, and finally deposited in the Sydenham Crystal Palace, England, only to be burned in the fire which destroyed a part of that building some years since. The two trees thus destroyed were among the finest, if not the very finest in the grove. Among those now standing, the tallest is the "Keystone State;" the largest and finest, the "Empire State."

The following table gives the height of all the trees measured by the State Survey, and their girth six feet from the ground:

Names of Trees.	Girth.	Height.
Keystone State	45	325
General Jackson	40	319
Mother of the Forest (without bark)	61	315
Daniel Webster	47	307
Richard Cobden	41	284
Starr King	52	283
Pride of the Forest	48	282
Henry Clay	47	280
Bay State	46	275
Jas. King of William	51	274
Sentinel	49	272
Dr. Kane	50	271
Arbor Vitae Queen	30	269
Abraham Lincoln	44	268
Maid of Honor	27	266
Old Vermont	40	265
Uncle Sam	43	265
Mother (and Son)	51	264
Three Graces (highest)	30	262
Wm. Cullen Bryant	48	262
U. S. Grant	34	261
Gen. Scott	43	258
Geo. Washington	51	256
Henry Ward Beecher	34	252
California	33	250
Uncle Tom's Cabin	50	250
Beauty of the Forest	39	249
J. B. McPherson	31	246
Florence Nightingale	37	246
James Wadsworth	27	239
Elihu Burritt	31	231

The exact measurement of the diameter and the ascertaining of the age of one of the largest trees in this grove, was accomplished by cutting it down. This was done soon after the discovery of the grove. It occupied five men during twenty-two days. They did it by boring into the tree with pump augers. The tree stood so perfectly vertical that, even after they had bored it completely off, it would not fall. It took three days' labor driving huge wedges in upon one side until the monumental monster leaned, toppled and fell.

They hewed and smoothed off the stump six feet above the ground, and then made careful measurements as follows:

Across its longest diameter, north of centre, 10 feet 4 inches.
Across its longest diameter, south of centre, 13 " 9½ "

Total largest diameter, 24 feet 1½ inc's.

The shorter diameter, from east to west, was twenty-three feet, divided exactly even, eleven and one half feet from the centre each way.

The thickness of the bark averaged eighteen inches. This would add three feet to the diameter, making the total diameter as the tree originally stood, a little over twenty-seven feet one way, and twenty-six feet the other. That is *eighty-five feet in circumference, six feet from the ground.*

The age was ascertained thus: After it had been felled, it was again cut through about thirty feet from the first cut. At the upper end of this section, which was, of course, nearly forty feet above the ground, as the tree originally stood, they carefully counted the rings of annual growth, at the same time exactly measuring the width of each set of one hundred rings, counting from the outside inwards.

These were the figures:

First hundred rings	3.0 inches.
Second " "	3.7 "
Third " "	4.1 "
Fourth " "	3.9 "
Fifth " "	4.1 "
Sixth " "	4.1 "
Seventh " "	4.6 "
Eighth " "	5.6 "
Ninth " "	7.3 "
Tenth " "	7.9 "
Eleventh " "	10.1 "
Twelfth " "	13.0 "
Fifty-five years	9.4 "
1,255 years.	80.8 inches.

A small hole in the middle of the tree prevented the exact determining of the number of rings which had rotted away, or were missing from the centre; but allowing for that, as well as for the time which the tree must have taken to grow to the height at which they made the count, it is probably speaking within bounds, to say that this tree was, in round numbers, thirteen hundred years old!

As the table shows, this grove contains four trees over three hundred feet high. The heights of these big trees, in both the great groves, are usually overstated. The above measurements were carefully and scientifically made—in several cases repeated and verified—and may be relied on as correct.

The "Keystone State" enjoys the proud honor of lifting its head higher than any other tree now known to be standing on the western continent. Australia has trees a hundred and fifty feet higher. The stories occasionally told of trees over four hundred feet high having once stood in this grove, have no reasonable foundation and are not entitled to belief. Neither is it true, as some have marvelously asserted, that it takes two men and a boy, working half a day each, to look to the top of the highest tree in this grove.

The Calaveras trees, as a rule, are taller and slimmer than those of Mariposa. This has probably resulted from their growing in a spot more sheltered from the high winds which sweep across the Sierra, to which other groves have been more exposed.

The Mariposa Grove,

likewise named from the county in which it stands, is about sixteen miles directly south of the lower hotel in Yosemite valley, and about four miles southeast of Clark's Ranch. Like the Calaveras Grove, it occupies a shallow valley or depression in the back of a ridge which runs easterly between Big Creek and the South Merced. One branch of the creek rises in the grove.

The grant made by Congress is two miles square and embraces two distinct groves; that is, two collections of big trees, separated by a considerable space having none. The upper grove contains three hundred and sixty-five trees of the true *Sequoia Gigantea* species, having a diameter of one foot or over. Besides these, are a great number of younger and smaller ones.

The lower grove is not as large, and its trees are more scattered. It lies southwesterly from the upper. Some of its trees grow quite high up the gulches on the south side of the ridge which separates the two groves.

On Wednesday, July 7th, 1869, the largest trees of this grove were carefully measured, under the guidance and with the assistance of Mr. Clarke himself, one of the State Commissioners charged with the care of these groves and of the Yosemite valley. To prevent misunderstanding and insure uniformity, each tree was measured three feet from the ground, except where the outside of the base was burned away, when the tree was girted seven and a half feet above ground.

The following figures are taken from that day's phonographic journal, written on the spot:

The "Grizzly Giant," seven and one half feet up, measures seventy-eight and one half feet in circumference. Three feet above ground this tree measured over a hundred feet round; but several feet of this measurement came from projecting roots, where they swell out from the trunk into the mammoth diagonal braces or shores, necessary to support and stiffen such a gigantic structure in its hold upon the earth.

One hundred feet up, an immense branch, over six feet through, grows out horizontally some twenty feet, then turns like an elbow and goes up forty feet. It naturally suggests some huge gladiator, uncovering his biceps and drawing up his arm to "show his muscle." This is the largest tree now standing in the grove, and is the one of which Starr King wrote:

"I confess that my own feeling, as I first scanned it, and let the eye roam up its tawny pillar, was of intense disappointment. But then, I said to myself, this is, doubtless, one of the striplings of this Anak brood—only a small affair of some forty feet in girth. I took out the measuring line, fastened it on the trunk with a knife, and walked around, unwinding as I went. The line was seventy-five feet long. I came to the end before completing the circuit. Nine feet more were needed. I had dismounted before a structure *eighty-four feet* in circumference, and nearly three hundred feet high, and I should not have guessed that it would measure more than fifteen feet through."

Here, as in Yosemite and at Niagara, tourists are usually disappointed in the first view. The lifelong familiarity with lesser magnitudes makes it almost impossible for the mind to free itself from the trammels of habit, and leap at a single bound, into any adequate perception of the incredible magnitudes which confront him. One needs spend at least a week among these Brobdignagian bulks, come twice a day and stay twelve hours each time, before he grows to any worthy appreciation of their unbelievable bigness.

Of the other trees, the largest ten, measured three feet above ground, gave the following circumferences:

La Fayette	83 feet.
The Governor	75 "
Chas. Crocker	75 "
The Chief Commissioner	74 "
Governor Stanford	74 "
Washington	72 "
Pluto's Chimney	71 "
The Big Diamond (Koh-i-noor)	65 "
The Governor's Wife	62 "
The Forest Queen	58 "

Others of equal size, possibly greater than some above, were not measured.

"The Governor" is a generic name, applied in honor of him who may happen to be the actual incumbent at any time. At present, of course, it means Gov. Haight. It is an actual botanical fact, that the tree has actually *gained* in *height* under the present gubernatorial administration. It certainly is not as *low*(e) by several inches as during the reign, or lack of rain, of the preceding incumbent.

The same general complimentary intention christened the "Governor's Wife," which has as graceful a form and as dignified a bearing among trees as such a lady should have among the women of the State. Then, too, the tree stands with a gentle inclination toward "The Governor," which may not be without its suggestions to those fond of tracing analogies.

The "Chief Commissioner" is the largest of a clump of eight, which stand grouped, as if in consultation, at a respectful distance from the Governor.

"Pluto's Chimney" is a huge old stump, burned and blackened all over, inside and out. Hibernian visitors sometimes call it "The Devil's Dhudeen." It is between forty and fifty feet high. On one side of the base is a huge opening, much like a a Puritan fireplace or a Scotch inglenook; while within, the whole tree is burned away so that one can look up and out clear to the very sky through its huge circular chimney. Outside, the bark and the roots have been burned wholly away. Before the burning, this tree must have equaled the largest.

Nearly in front of the cabin in the upper grove, and not far from the delicious spring before alluded to, stands a solitary tree having its roots burned away on one side, leaning south, and presenting a general appearance of trying to "swing round the circle." In view of all these facts, some imaginative genius once christened it "Andy Johnson." The only inappropriate thing in the application of that name was the fact that the tree stood so near a spring of cold water. The "Big Diamond" or "Koh-i-noor" is the largest of a group of four very straight and symmetrical trees occupying the corners of a regular rhombus or lozenge, so exactly drawn as to readily suggest the name "Diamond Group," by which they have been called.

As already remarked, the Mariposa Grove really consists of two groves—the upper and the lower, which approach within a half mile of each other. The upper grove contains three hundred and sixty-five trees; one for every day in the year, with large ones for Sundays. By an unfortunate omission, however, it makes no provision for leap year. This is the principal objection which unmarried spinster tourists have thus far been able to urge against it.

The lower grove has two hundred and forty-one trees, generally smaller than those of the upper grove. The total number in both groves, according to the latest official count, is six hundred and six.

Within ten years several trees have fallen, and others follow them from time to time, so that the most accurate count of them made in any one year might not tally with another equally careful count a year earlier or later.

Among the prostrate trees lies the "Fallen Giant," measuring eighty-five feet around, three feet from the present base. The bark, the sapwood, the roots, and probably the original base, are all burned away. When standing, this monster must have been by far the largest in both groves, and, indeed, larger than any now known in the world. It should have been called "Lucifer," a name hereby respectfully submitted for the consideration of future tourists.

The living trees of this species exude a dark-colored substance, looking like gum, but readily dissolving in water. This has a very acrid, bitter taste, which probably aids in preserving the tree from injurious insects, and preventing the decay of the woody fibre.

The fruit or seed is hardly conical, but rather ellipsoidal or rudely oval in form, an inch and a half long by one inch through, and looking far too insignificant to contain the actual germ of the most gigantic structure known to botanical science.

Their age, indicated by the concentric rings of annual growth, carefully counted and registered by the gentlemen of the State Survey, varies from five to thirteen, possibly fifteen, centuries.

The word "*Sequoia*," is the Latin form of the Indian *Sequoyah*, the name of a Cherokee Indian of mixed blood, who is supposed to have been born about 1770, and who lived in Will's Valley, in the extreme northeastern corner of Alabama, among the Cherokees. His English name was George Guess. He became famous by his invention of an alphabet, and written letters for his tribe. This alphabet was constructed with wonderful ingenuity. It consisted of eighty-six characters, each representing a syllable, and it had already come into considerable use before the whites heard anything of it. After a while, the missionaries took up Sequoyah's idea, had types cast, supplied a printing press to the Cherokee nation, and in 1828 started a newspaper printed partly with these types. Driven, with the rest of his tribe, beyond the Mississippi, he died in New Mexico, in 1843. His alphabet is still in use, though destined to pass away with his doomed race, but not into complete oblivion, for his name, attached to one of the grandest productions of the vegetable kingdom will keep his memory forever green.

For the foregoing bit of aboriginal biography, we gratefully acknowledge our obligation to Prof. Brewer and the gentlemen of the State Survey, to whom he originally furnished it.

Had Sequoyah's name been Cadmus—had the Cherokees been Phenicians—and had this modern heathen of the eighteenth century invented his alphabet away back before the Christian era, his name would have stood in every school history among those of inventors, philosophers, discoverers and benefactors; as it is he's "only an Indian." No one can deny, however, that he was one of the best re(a)d men in the history of the world.

Both the Calaveras and the Mariposa groves contain hollow trunks of fallen trees, through which, or into which, two and even three horsemen can ride abreast for sixty or seventy feet. Each grove, also, has trees which have been burned out at the base, but have not fallen. Still standing, they contain or enclose huge charcoal-lined rooms, into which one can ride. The writer has been one of four mounted men who rode their horses into such a cavity in the Mariposa grove, and reined their horses up side by side without crowding each other or pressing the outside one against the wall.

One who has seen only the ordinary big trees of "down east," or "out west," forests, finds it hard to believe that any such vegetable monsters can really exist. Even the multiplied and repeated assurances of friends who have actually "*seen* them, sir," and "measured them *myself*, I tell you," hardly arrest the outward expression of incredulity, and seldom win the inward faith of the skeptical hearer. Fancy yourself sitting down to an after-dinner chat in the fifteen-foot sitting room, adjoining the dining room of equal size. You fall to talking of the "Big Trees." You say, "Why, my dear sir, I have actually rode into, and sat upon my horse in, a tree whose hollow was so big that you could put both these rooms into it, side by side, and still have seven or eight feet of solid wood standing on each side of me. . No, sir, not romancing at *all*. It's an actual, scientific, measured *fact*, sir." Your friend looks quizzically and incredulously into both your eyes, as he says, "Why, now see here, my dear fellow, do you suppose I'm going to believe that? Tell a *moderate* whopper, and back it up with such repeated assertion and scientific authority, and you might possibly make me believe it, or at least, allow it until you were fairly out of hearing; but to sit here at a man's own fireside and tell him such a *monstrous* story as that, and expect him to swallow it for truth—ah, no, my dear fellow, that's *too* much, altogether too much."

So you have to give it over and drop the argument for the present, in the hope that some one of the numerous excursion parties, now so rapidly multiplying every year, will soon include him, carry him into the actual presence of these veritable monsters of the vegetable kingdom, confront him with their colossal columns, and compel his belief.

And yet the general incredulity is hardly to be wondered at, after all. In nearly every one of us, our faith in what *may* be, largely depends upon our personal knowledge of the *facts* which *have* been. In matters pertaining to the outward, the material, the physical world, our actual experience of the past governs our belief as to the future. And even when the objects of our disbelief are set bodily before our vision, and we have actually seen them and handled them, it is often difficult to believe our own eyes. So far is "seeing from believing" when the sight so far surpasses all former experience.

There is another grove of big trees in Fresno county, about fourteen miles southeast of Clark's. It is not far from a conspicuous point called Wammelo Rock. The State Survey did not include it, neither have tourists usually visited it. According to the description of Mr. Clark, who has partially explored it, it extends for more than two miles and a half in length, by from one to two in width. He has counted five hundred trees in it, and believes it to contain not far from six hundred in all. The largest which he measured had a circumference of eighty-one feet at three feet from the ground.

Following along the slope of the Sierras, to the southeast about fifty miles, between King's and Kaweah rivers, we find the largest grove of these trees yet discovered in the State.

The State Survey partially explored this locality, and have given us the following particulars: The trees form a belt rather than a grove. This belt is found about thirty miles north-northeast of Visalia, near the tributaries of the King's and Kaweah rivers, and along the divide between. They are scattered up and down the slopes and along the valleys, but reach their greatest size in the shallow basins where the soil is more moist.

Along the trail from Visalia to Big Meadows the belt is four or five miles wide and extends through a vertical range of twenty-five hundred feet; that is, the trees along the lower edge of the belt stand nearly half a mile in perpendicular height below those along its upper boundary. The length of this belt is as much as eight or ten miles and may be more.

These trees are not collected in groves, but straggle along through the forests in company with the other species usually found at this height in the Sierras. They are most abundant between six and seven thousand feet above the sea. Their number is very great; probably thousands might be counted. In size, however, they are not remarkable; that is, in comparison with those of Calaveras and Mariposa. But few exceed twenty feet in diameter—the average is from ten to twelve feet, while the great majority are smaller.

One tree which had been felled, had a diameter of eight feet, not including the bark, and was three hundred and seventy-seven years old. The largest one seen was near Thomas' Mill. This had a circumference of one hundred and six feet near the ground, though quite a portion of the base had been burned away.

Another tree, which had fallen and been burned

hollow, was so large that three horsemen could ride abreast into the cavity for thirty feet, its inside height and width being nearly twelve feet. Seventy feet in, the diameter of the cavity was still as much as eight feet.

The base of this tree could not be easily measured; but the trunk was burned off at one hundred and twenty feet from the base, and at that point had a diameter, not including the bark, of thirteen feet and two inches. At one hundred and sixty-nine feet from its base, this tree was still nine feet through. The Indians speak of a still larger tree to the north of King's river. It was not in the power of the State Survey to look it up and measure it at that time.

All through these forests young Big Trees of all sizes, from the seedling upwards, were very numerous. At Thomas' Mill they cut them up into lumber, as if they were the most common tree in the forest.

Fallen trunks of old trees are also numerous. Many of these must have lain for ages, as they had almost wholly rotted away, though the wood is very durable.

Judging from the number of these trees found between King's and Kaweah rivers, it would seem that the Big Trees best like that locality and its vicinity, so that it is not improbable that a further exploration would show a continuous belt of some fifty or sixty miles in extent.

From the researches thus far made, it appears that the Big Tree is not as strange and exceptional as most suppose. It occurs in such abundance, of all ages and sizes, that there is no reason to conclude that it is dying out, or that it belongs exclusively to some past geological or botanical epoch. The age of the big trees is not as great as that assigned by some of the highest authorities to some of the English yews. And in height they hardly begin to equal that of the Australian *Eucalyptus amygdalina*, many of which, on the authority of Dr. Muller, the eminent Government botanist, have exceeded four hundred feet. One, indeed, reached the enormous height of *four hundred and eighty feet*, thus overtopping the tallest *Sequoia* by one hundred and fifty-five feet. And in diameter, also, there are trees which exceed the Big Tree, as, for example, the *Baobab*; but these are always comparatively low, rarely reaching the height of more than sixty or seventy feet, while their excessive diameter comes from a peculiarly swollen and distorted base. On the whole, we may safely claim that no known tree in the world equals the California Big Trees in the combined elements of size and height, and in consequent grandeur, unless, indeed, it may be the *Eucalyptus*. The largest Australian tree yet reported, is said to be eighty-one feet in circumference, four feet from the ground. This is a highly respectable vegetable, but not quite equal to the certified measurements of some of the largest of the California Big Trees.

So the American tourist through the wonders of California, may yet claim that his country still possesses the loftiest waterfalls, the most overpowering cliffs, and the grandest trees yet known upon the face of the globe.

BOWER CAVE.

The traveler who desires good roads, romantic scenery, comfortable conveyances, and excellent hotel accommodations, will be sure to go in or come out by way of Coulterville. This town lies on Maxwell creek, a branch of the Merced, about eighteen hundred feet above the sea, and not far from the border-land between the "foot-hills" and the mountains proper. The road runs from Coulterville nearly northeast, about eight miles, when it strikes the North Fork of the Merced. Along the side of this stream it descends for a short distance, then crosses and passes near the

Bower Cave.

This is a picturesque and unique locality, and is well worth a visit.

The cave is an immense crack or sink, or both combined, in the solid limestone of the mountain-top. At the surface it presents a somewhat crescent-shaped opening, one hundred and thirty-three feet long, eighty-six feet wide near the centre, and one hundred and nine feet deep in the deepest place. Trees grow from the bottom and lift their branches out through the opening at the top, while a beautifully tranquil and wonderfully clear lake occupies the greater portion of the floor.

We enter at the north end and go down by a rough but strong and safe staircase. The walls of the cleft are perpendicular, or nearly so, thoughout the greater portion of their extent, but near the south end the upper part of the wall projects or overhangs several feet.

The bottom has the form of an irregular square, measuring over a hundred feet one way and somewhat less than a hundred the other. From the bottom and near the centre grow three large maples, the largest of which is more than two feet through, and about a hundred and twenty-five feet high. Around these trees are benches, capable of seating a score or two of persons. On one side of the wall, some twenty feet above the bottom, is a singular niche or alcove which has been christened the "Pulpit." It is occasionally used for the legitimate purpose of similar constructions, though more frequently occupied by the fiddler of some festive party. Upon special occasions, such as a Fourth of July celebration, they erect tables here and use all the available floor as a dining hall. Over a hundred have thus dined here at one time.

In one corner, and nearly under the pulpit, is a

small but singularly beautiful lake, rendered somewhat ghostly and mysterious by the overhanging rocky wall, and the intercepted light falling through the overshadowing trees. Upon this lake is a small boat, in which the imaginative visitor may easily fancy himself crossing the Styx, with himself as his own Charon. Not far from the corner of this lake, nearly under the pulpit, the water is claimed to have an immense depth. In all parts it is so clear that one can plainly see the cracks and crevices in the sloping limestone sides at the depth of forty feet. The vision would, doubtless, penetrate much deeper did not the overhanging walls obstruct the light.

Having rowed across the lake, as you are returning to the shore, the guide may possibly ask you to keep very quiet while he calls and feeds his fish. He gives a few soft whistles, places his hand in the water, waits a moment, repeats his whistle, and softly whispers, "Here they come." Up swim several large trout, rub their noses against his hand, and circle slowly around it, evidently waiting for the customary food. And that hand seldom disappoints them. It is a pleasant and restful sight. After enjoying it, seeing them finish feeding, and returning to the landing, you ask the guide how they became so tame. He tells you, that for several weeks after putting them into the lake, which he did some years ago, he came every day, about the same time, softly whistling and gently dropping crumbs and worms into the water. After a few days he began to hold on to one end of a worm while the trout would swim up, take hold of the other end and tug away until he pulled it apart, or the hand let go. After a few months they seemed to have learned to associate the whistling and the feeding, so that whenever they hear the first they swim up in evident expectation of the second.

At various heights upon one wall several large cavities or small caves are worn into the rock, some of which admit the tourist for a considerable distance. These make that side of the wall a collection of cells, some of which are high enough to permit the visitor to walk erect; others so low that they compel one who would enter to crawl upon his hands and knees. When first discovered, the walls of these chambers were covered with beautiful stalactites of various sizes and fanciful forms, but the ruthless hands of vandal visitors have gradually broken them off and carried them away, until hardly a trace of their original beauty and variety remains.

During the heat of the summer, the time when nearly all visitors enter this cave, its cool and refreshing temperature makes it a comfortable and welcome retreat, especially during the hotter midday hours. The place seems as if nature and art had combined to make it as attractive as possible for hot weather picnics, or midsummer lunch parties. It is difficult to imagine, and almost impossible to discover a more fascinating combination of dell and grotto, grove and lake, cave and bower, than nature has kindly provided for the tourist in the romantic Bower Cave.

ALABASTER CAVE.

The following account of one of the most beautiful of all nature's marvels, is taken, with few alterations, from Yosemite Hutchings' book, entitled "Scenes of Wonder and Curiosity in California."

The Alabaster Cave is in El Dorado County, twelve and a half miles from Folsom by the "Whisky Bar" road, and ten miles by the El Dorado Valley turnpike. Its more exact location is upon Kidd's Ravine, about three quarters of a mile from its opening upon the north fork of the American River. From Sacramento it is thirty-three miles; by rail to Folsom: from Auburn, about three miles, by stage.

It was discovered in April, 1860, in the following way: A ledge of limestone, resembling marble in appearance, cropped out by the side of El Dorado Valley turnpike road. Upon testing it was found to be capable of producing excellent lime.

On the 18th of April, 1860, two workmen, George S. Hatterman and John Harris, were quarrying limestone from this ledge, when, upon the removal of a large piece of rock, they discovered a dark opening sufficiently enlarged to permit their entrance. Availing themselves of the light pouring in through the opening, they went in as far as they could see—some fifty feet. Before venturing further into the darkness, they threw a stone forward, which, striking in water, determined them to return for lights. At this juncture Mr. Gwinn, the owner of the ledge, came up, and, upon learning of their discovery, immediately sent for candles to enable them to further prosecute their explorations. The result of these, after several hours spent in them, can hardly be better described than in Mr. Gwinn's own language, taken from a letter, dated April 19, 1860, addressed to Mr. Holmes, a gentleman friend of his residing in Sacramento, and first published in the *Bee*, of that city:

"Wonders will never cease. On yesterday, we, in quarrying rock, made an opening to the most beautiful cave you ever beheld. On our first entrance we descended about fifteen feet, gradually, to the centre of the room, which is one hundred by thirty feet. At the north end there is a most magnificent pulpit, in the Episcopal church style, that man has ever seen. It seems that it is, and should be, called the "Holy of Holies." It is completed with the most beautiful drapery of alabaster sterites of all colors, varying from white to pink-red, overhanging the beholder. Immediately under the pulpit there is a beautiful lake of water, extending to an unknown distance. We thought this all, but, to our great admiration, on arriving at the centre of the first room, we saw an entrance to an inner chamber, still more splendid; two hundred by one hundred feet, with the most beautiful alabaster overhanging in every possible shape of drapery. Here stands magnitude, giving the instant impression of a power above man; grandeur that defies decay; antiquity that tells of ages *unnumbered;* beauty that the touch of time makes more beautiful; use exhaustless for the service of men; strength imperishable as the globe; the monument of eternity—the truest earthly emblem of that everlasting and unchangeable, irresistible Majesty, by whom, and for whom, all things were made."

As soon as the news spread, hundreds of people flocked to see the newly discovered wonder, from all the surrounding mining settlements, so that within the first six days, it was visited by upwards of four hundred persons, many of whom, we regret to say, possessed a larger organ of acquisitiveness than of veneration, and laid vandal hands on some of the most beautiful portions within reach, near the entrance. Upon this, the proprietor closed it until arrangements could be made for its protection and systematic illumination; the better to see and not to touch the specimens.

At this time Messrs. Smith & Hatterman leased the cave and immediately began to prepare it for the reception of the public by building barricades, platforms, etc., and placing a large number of lamps at favorable points, for the better illumination and inspection of the different chambers.

At the time of its discovery, in the spring, considerable water was standing in some of the deepest of the cavities, but it presently began to recede at the rate of nearly six inches a day, and continued to do so, until, in a few weeks, it had entirely disappeared, leaving the cave perfectly dry. This afforded opportunity for further exploration, upon which it was found that a more convenient entrance could be made, with but little labor, from an unimportant room within a few feet of the road. This was accordingly done, and the new opening, in addition to its increased convenience, allows the free circulation of pure air.

Having thus given a historical sketch of its discovery, with other matters connected with its preservation and management, we shall now endeavor to take the reader with us, at least in imagination, while attempting a detailed description of its interior.

Upon approaching the cave from the roadside, we descend three or four steps to a board floor. Here is a door which is always carefully locked when no visitors are within. Passing on we enter a chamber about twenty-five feet long by seventeen feet wide and from five to twelve and a half feet in height.

Though very plain and comparatively unattractive at both roof and sides, it is yet quite curious, especially to visitors unaccustomed to caves. Here is also a desk, upon which lies a book inscribed, "Coral Cave Register." This book was presented by some gentlemen of San Francisco, who thought that the name "Coral Cave" would be more appropriate. The impression produced upon our mind upon the first walk through it, was that "Alabaster Cave" would be equally as good a name, but, upon examining it more thoroughly, we afterwards thought, that as a great proportion of the ornaments at the roots of the stalactites look like beautifully frozen mosses, or very fine coral, and the long icicle-looking pendants being more like alabaster, the name, Coral Cave, was to be preferred. But as Mr. Gwinn had given the name "Alabaster" to the works themselves, on account of the purity and whiteness of the limestone there found, even before the discovery of the cave, we cheerfully acquiesce in the name originally given.

The register was opened April twenty-fourth, 1860, and upon our visit, September thirtieth of the same year, two thousand seven hundred and twenty-one names had been registered. Some three or four thousand persons had visited it before the register was provided, many declined entering their names after it was furnished, and many others visited it after the date of our visit, so that it is probable that the number of persons who entered this cave during the year of its discovery must have been nearly or quite three thousand five hundred.

Advancing beyond the vestibule, or register room, along another passage or room, our eyes rest on several notices, such as, "Please not touch the specimens." "No smoking allowed," "Hands and feet off," with *feet* scratched out, amputation of those members not intended!

The low, shelving, rocky wall upon the left and near the end of the passage are covered with coral-like excrescences, resembling bunches of coarse rock-moss. This brings us to the entrance of the

Dungeon of Enchantment.

Before us is a broad, oddly-shaped and low-roofed chamber, about one hundred and twenty feet long, by seventy in width, and from four to twenty feet high.

Bright coral-like stalactites hang down in irregular rows and in almost every variety of shape and shade, from milk-white to cream color; forming a most agreeable contrast with the dark arches and the frowning buttresses on either hand, while low-browed ridges, some almost black, others of a reddish-brown, stretch from either side, the space between which is ornamented with a peculiar kind of coloring which nearly resembles a grotesque species of graining.

Descending toward the left, we approach one of the most singularly beautiful groups of stalactites in this apartment. Some of these are fine pendants, hardly larger than pipestems, from two to five feet long, and hollow from end to end. When the cave was first discovered there were four or five of these pendants over eight feet long, but the early admitted vandals ruthlessly destroyed, or selfishly carried them off. Others resemble the ears of white elephants, or, rather, the white elephant of Siam, while others still present the appearance of long and slender cones, inverted.

Examining this and other groups more closely, we discover at their bases coral-like excrescences of great beauty; here, like petrified moss, brilliant, and almost transparent; there, a pretty fungus, tipped and spangled with diamonds; yonder, miniature pine trees, which, with a most obliging disposition to accommodate themselves to circumstances, grow bottom up. In other places appear fleeces of the finest merino or silky floss.

Leaving these, and turning to the right, we can ascend a ladder into the loftiest part of this chamber. Here new combinations of beauty surprise and delight us. Thence passing on, we come to a large stalagmite, whose form and size suggest a tying post for horses. This has been dignified, or mystified, anything but beautified, by different names, more or less appropriate. One is "Lot's

Wife." If the woman was no higher than the staglamite, she must have been a dwarf, for the top of the post is but four feet and a quarter above its bottom, while its diameter at the bottom is hardly one foot. Its two other names, "Hercules' Club," and "Brobdignag's Forefinger," are more appropriate, though the latter would suggest an "exaggeration," as Mrs. Partington would have it.

Continuing on, we pass over a gently rising floor resembling solidified snow, until we approach the verge of, and look down into, an immense abyss, surmounted by a cavernous roof. Icicle and coral formations depend from the roof, and a rude drapery of jet covers the sides. Here is suspended a singular petrifaction resembling a human heart, which which looks as if it might have belonged to one of the primitive Titans, or come from the chest of that Miltonian monster, whose spear-shaft was like a Norway pine.

On one side of this is an elevated and nearly level natural floor, upon which a table and seats have been temporarily erected for the convenience of choristers, choirs or singing societies, and even for the accommodation of public worship, should any desire to witness or participate in it in this most beautiful of God's natural temples. The lover of sacred music would be delighted beyond measure to hear these "vaulted hills" resound the symphonies of Mozart, Haydn or Mendelssohn. Scores of these pendent harps would vibrate in unison, or echo them in delicious harmonies from chamber to chamber, or bear them from roof to wall in diminishing reverberations even to the most remote of these rock-formed corridors.

We may not linger here too long, so passing hence, we enter other and smaller chambers, along whose roofs we trace formations that resemble streams of water suddenly arrested in their flow and turned to ice. In another, a peculiarly shaped petrifaction presents a perfectly formed beet from one point of view, while from another it resembles a small elephant's head. Not far hence, a bell-shaped hollow, a beautiful combination of grotto and arcade, has received the name of "Julia's Bower."

Once more advancing, a narrow, low-roofed passage brings us into the most beautiful chamber of all, the

Crystal Chapel.

No language can suitably convey, nor any comparisons worthily suggest, the combined beauty and magnificence of this wonderful spot. "From the beginning," says Hutchings, "we have felt that we were almost presumptuous in attempting to portray these wonderful scenes, but, in hope of inducing others to see, with their natural eyes, the sights that we have seen, and enjoy the pleasure that we have enjoyed, we entered upon the task, even though inadequately, of giving an outline—nothing more. Here, however, we confess ourselves entirely at a loss.

"The sublime grandeur of this imposing sight fills the soul with astonishment that swells up from within as though its purpose was to make the beholder speechless, the language of silence being the most fitting and impressive when puny man treads the great halls of nature, the more surely to lead him, humbly, from these to the untold glory of the Infinite One who devised the laws, and superintended the processes that brought such wonders into being.

"After the mind seems prepared to examine this gorgeous spectacle somewhat in detail, we look upon the ceiling, if we may so speak, which is entirely covered with myriads of the most beautiful of stone icicles, long, large and brilliant; between these are squares or panels, the mullions and bars of which seem to be formed of diamonds; while the panels themselves resemble the frosting upon windows in the very depth of winter; and even those are of many colors, that most prevailing being of a light pinkish-cream. Moss, coral, floss, wool, trees, and many other forms, adorn the interstices between the larger of the stalactites. At the further end is one vast mass of rock, resembling congealed water, apparently formed into many folds and hillocks; in many instances connected by pillars with the roof above. Deep down and underneath this is the entrance by which we reached the chamber.

"At our right stands a large staglamite, dome-shaped at the top, and covered with beautifully undulating and wavy folds. Every imaginable gracefulness possible to the most curiously arranged drapery, is here visible, 'carved in alabaster' by the Great Architect of the universe. This is named 'The Pulpit.'

"In order to examine this object with more minuteness, a temporary platform has been erected, which, although detractive of the general effect, in our opinion, affords a nearer and better view of all these remarkable objects in detail.

"This spectacle, as well as the others, being brilliantly illuminated, the scene is very imposing, and reminds one of those highly-wrought pictures of the imagination, painted in such charming language and with such good effect in such works as the 'Arabian Nights.'

"Other apartments known as the 'Picture Gallery,' etc., might well detain us longer, but, as in many of their most important particulars, they bear a striking resemblance to those already described, we leave them for the tourist to examine for himself." If what we have said excites the desire of any tourist to visit this new combination of wonder and beauty, we are quite sure he will agree with us that the words of man utterly fail to adequately picture forth the works of God, and will ever after delight his soul with the life-long memory of his charming visit to the wonderful Alabaster Cave.

Tourist's Complete Guide

TO

San Francisco, Suburbs and Vicinity;

WITH SPECIAL TRIPS AND SHORT EXCURSIONS IN AND ABOUT THE CITY.

I. CITY PROPER.

SKETCH OF THE CITY—Historical, Topographical, General Plan - - - - - - - - - 95–107
APPROACHES TO THE CITY—From the east, by boat; from the south, by rail; from the ocean, by steamship, 107–113
CONVEYANCES—Hacks, Coaches, Cars, Porters, Legal Rates, Caution, Baggage and Package Express, - - 113–116
HOTELS—Grand, Occidental, Cosmopolitan, Lick House, Brooklyn, Russ House, American Exchange, Morton House, International, Hotel Gailhard, What Cheer, (males only), - - - - - - - 116–121
LODGING HOUSES—Nucleus, Clarendon, - - - 121
RESTAURANTS—Saulman's, Swain's, Job's, Martin's, Lermitte's, - - - - - - - - 121–122
BATHS—Fresh, Salt, Turkish, Russian, Roman, Steam and Vapor, - - - - - - - - - 122
PLACES OF AMUSEMENT—California, Metropolitan, Alhambra, Maguire's, and Chinese Theatres; Museums, Melodeons, Dance Halls, and Beer Cellars, - - 122–125
HALLS—Platt's, Union, Pacific, Mercantile Library, Mechanic's Institute, Y. M. C. A., Mozart, Dashaway, 125–126
BILLIARDS, Bowling Saloons and Shooting Galleries, 127–128

GYMNASIUMS—Olympic Club, Y. M. C. A., German Turn
Verein, Skating Rinks, Base Ball Ground, - 128–130
GARDENS—Woodward's, City, - - - - 130–140
MENAGERIES—Woodward's Zoological Grounds, North
Beach, - - - - - - - - - 140
SQUARES AND PARKS—Plaza, (Portsmouth Square). Washington Square, South Park, - - - - 141
PROMENADES—Montgomery Street, Kearny Street, California Street. BEST TIME, - - - - 141–144
DRIVES—Cliff House Road, Ocean House Road, Bay View, New Ocean Road, Best Time, - - - - 145–148
LIBRARIES AND READING ROOMS—Mercantile, Mechanic's Institute, Odd Fellow's, Pioneers, Y. M. C. A., What Cheer, Woodward's Gardens, - - - - - 148
PUBLIC BUILDINGS—*Federal:* Post Office, Custom House, Old Mint, New Mint, Marine Hospital. *City and County:* Old City Hall, New City Hall, Jail, Almshouse, Industrial School, Engine Houses, Engines. *Corporation and Society Buildings:* Pioneer's, Merchant's Exchange, Bank of California, Mercantile Library Building, Mechanic's Institute, Masonic Temple, Odd Fellow's Hall, Y. M. C. A. Building, Mechanics' Pavilion, - - - 148–157
BUSINESS BUILDINGS AND BLOCKS—Alta California Building, Bancroft's, Donohoe, Kelly & Co., Harpending's Block, Murphy, Grant & Co., Tobin, Dixon & Davisson, Treadwell's, Tucker's, Wells, Fargo & C.'s Building, White House, - - - - - - - - 157–159
MANUFACTORIES—Kimball Car and Carriage Factory, Pacific Rolling Mills, Mission Woolen Mills, Foundries and Iron Works, Locomotives, Boilers, Mining Machinery, Shot Tower and Lead Works, Sugar Refinery, Glass Works, Ship Yards, - - - - - - 159–161
CHURCHES—Baptist, Congregational, Episcopal, Jewish, Methodist, Presbyterian, Roman Catholic, Swedenborgian, Unitarian, Chinese Mission House, Mariner's Church, Old Mission Church, - - - - 161–167
HOSPITALS AND ASYLUMS—City and County, French, German, Protestant Orphan, Roman Catholic Orphan, 167–169
COLLEGES—California Business University, City College, St. Ignatius', St. Mary's, Toland Medical, - 169–170

SCHOOL BUILDINGS—Denman, Girl's High, Lincoln, Valencia Street, - - - - - - - 171–172
PRINTING, Lithographing, Binding, and Blank Book Manufacturing Establishment, - - - - - 172–173
PRIVATE RESIDENCES—Davis', Eldridges, Laidley's, Latham's, Bancroft's, Otis', Parrott's, Tallant's, Taylor's, Tobin's, - - - - - - - - - 174
POINTS OF OBSERVATION—Telegraph Hill, Russian Hill, Clay Street Hill, California Street Hill, Rincon Hill, Lone Mountain, Twin Peaks, Bernal Heights, U. S. Observatory. Views from each, - - - 174–184
HOW TO GET ABOUT—Horse Car Lines, Routes, Distances, Times, Fares, Buggies, Carriages, Coaches and Saddle Horses; qualities of, and charges for. Hacks, with rates of hire, - - - - - - - - 184–188

II. SUBURBS AND VICINITY.

COMMENCING at the foot of Market street, thence southward along or near the water front, continuing around the entire city and returning to the point of starting. Also, mentioning more distant points, visible to the spectator looking beyond the suburbs.

LUMBER YARDS; Wharves and Merchant Fleet; California and Oregon S. S. Co.'s Wharves and Ships; Black Diamond Coal Co.'s Pier; Rincon Point; U. S. Marine Hospital; P. M. S. S. Co.'s Piers, Docks, Sheds and Ships; Gas Works: C. P. R. R. Co,'s Freight Pier, Depot and Boat; Mission Bay; Mission Rock; U. S. Ship Anchorage; Steamboat Reserves; Long Bridge; Yacht Club and Boat-house, with Yachts; Potrero; Glass Works; Pacific Rolling Mill; Deep Cut; Islais Creek and Bridge; Rope Walk; Italian Fishing Fleet and Flakes; Celestial Ditto; South San Francisco; Catholic Orphan Asylum; Hunter's Point; Dry Dock; Bay View Race Course; Visitacion Point and Valley; San Bruno Road; New Butchertown; Ocean House Road; Lake Honda; Almshouse; Small Pox Hospital; Ocean House Race Track; Lake Merced; Ocean House; Pacific Beach; Seal Rocks; Cliff House; Farallones; Point Lobos; Signal Station;

Helmet Rock; Fort Point; Fort; Light-House; Golden Gate; Lime Point; Point Bonita; Mountain Lake; Lobos Creek: Presidio; Barracks; Parade Ground; Black Point; Pacific Woolen Mills; North Beach; Angel Island; Alcatraz; North Point; Sea Wall; Ferries, 188–196

III. HOW TO SEE THE CITY.

Under this head we suggest:

Morning, or half-day excursions, in and about the city and its suburbs.

I. IN AND ABOUT THE CITY.

1. Montgomery Street, Telegraph Hill, North Beach, Washington Square, The Plaza, City Hall, Kearny street, - - - - - - - - - 197
2. Chinese Quarter, - - - - - - - 197
3. Third street, South Park, Long Bridge, Potrero, South San Francisco, Dry Dock, - - - - - 201
4. Water Front, (south), Stewart street, P. M. S. S. Co.'s Docks and Mammoth Steamships, Foundries, Factories, Shot Tower, - - - - - - - - 202
5. Water Front, (north), Sea Wall, North Point, Warehouses and Clippers, Iron Ships, Bay and River Steamboats and Docks, - - - - - - - 202
6. Southwestern Suburbs, Mission street, Woodward's Gardens, Old Mission Church, Jewish Cemeteries, Woolen Mills, Howard street, - - - - - 202
7. Western Suburbs and Beyond Bush street, Laurel Hill, Lone Mountain Cemeteries, Cliff House Road, Race Track, Cliff House, Seal rocks, Pacific Beach, Ocean House, Road Track, Lake Honda, New Ocean Road, 203
8. Northwestern Suburbs and Beyond: Russian Hill, Spring Valley, Fort Point, Fortress, Lighthouse, Golden Gate, Presidio, Black Point, - - - - - 203

SAN FRANCISCO.

Historical.

The site of what is now the city of San Francisco was first permanently occupied by white men, September 17, 1776. The same year witnessed the entrenchment of a garrison and the establishment of a Mission.

San Francisco owes its origin to Catholic missionaries and Spanish soldiers. Father Junipero Serra led the missionaries—and virtually commanded the soldiers. The name San Francisco was given in honor of Saint Francis of Asisis, a city of Italy, the founder of the order of Franciscans to which Father Junipero belonged. The presidio, garrison or fort, was founded first, Sept. 17, and the mission about three weeks later, Oct. 9th. The site first chosen was near a small lagoon back of, that is, west of, what is now called Russian Hill, but the prevailing winds proved so high and bitter as to compel its early removal to the more sheltered spot, over a mile south, under the lee of high hills, and near the present Mission Creek. Here, at the head of what is now Center or Sixteenth Street, the old church still stands.

For nearly sixty years the mission stood, the nucleus of a little village of rude adobe houses, tenanted by a fluctuating population of Indians, Mexicans and Spanish—and the center of a military and religious authority, which upon more than one occasion made itself felt and feared for leagues around. The population rarely rose above four hundred and frequently fell to less than a hundred and fifty.

In 1835, Capt. W. A. Richardson put up the first pioneer dwelling, with rude wooden walls and sail-cloth roof. On the fourth of July of the next year, 1836, Jacob P. Leese finished the first frame house. This house stood where the St. Francis Hotel now stands, — on the southwest corner of Clay and Dupont streets, a single block west of the present City Hall. Leese had his store on the beach, which was where Montgomery and Commercial streets now intersect. Nearly seven solid blocks of made-land now stretch between where that old beach lay and the present water front. Other houses soon rose near that of Leese, and presently the villagers saw their little settlement fast approaching the dignity of a new town, and cast about to find a name. Nature caused it to spring out of the ground for them in the form of a species of aromatic mint, which, surrounding their dwellings, perfuming the morning air and supplying frequent and varied medicinal needs, had proved indeed, as the Spaniards called it, "Yerba Buena," the Good Herb. So the herb named the town, and the name "*stuck*," as the Californians say, for nearly a dozen years. During these years the houses grew in number, until 1847, when the town contained seventy-nine buildings,—thirty-one frame, twenty-six adobe, and the rest shanties—and these houses sheltered three hundred souls, or, at least, that number of bodies. On the 30th of January of that year, these three hundred dropped the old name Yerba Buena, and adopted the older one, which had belonged to the neighboring mission for nearly fourscore years. Thus the town also became San Francisco, and has ever since so remained. The first steamboat appeared in the bay, November 15th of the same year. In March, 1848, the houses had grown to two hundred, and the population to eight hundred and fifty. On the third of the next month, the first public school began.

New Year's Day, '49, the new city claimed a population of two thousand. Three days later the two previously published weekly papers merged into the Alta California, the earliest established of all newspapers now existing in the State.

The early miners were making from twenty to thirty dollars a day, getting "bags" of dust and "piles" of nuggets, and rushing down to "Frisco" to gamble it away. These were the "flush times" of the new city. Fresh eggs cost from seventy-five cents to one dollar apiece. For a beefsteak and a cup of coffee for breakfast one had to pay a dollar and a half, and a dinner cost him from two to ten or even twenty dollars, according to appetite and drinketite. Rough labor brought the old Congressional pay of eight dollars a day; draymen earned twenty dollars a day; and family "help" could hardly be had for forty, or even fifty, dollars a week. The great mass of the men lived in tents. Very few women had come, but those few were overwhelmed with attention; if one wished to cross the street in the rainy season, a score of brawny arms would fight for the privilege of gallantly wading through the sea of mud to carry her across the unpaved street.

Great fires came, four of them; the first the day before Chistmas, '49—it burned over a million dollars worth; the second, May 4th, '50—it destroyed three millions dollars worth. A little over a month later, June 14th, 1850, the most destructive fire the city ever saw left it poorer by four millions of dollars; and on the 17th of the next September the fourth fire consumed another half million. Nearly nine million dollars worth burned in less than nine months!

Business thrived immensely: In 1852, more than seven vessels a day arrived at or departed from San Francisco. Commerce overdid itself. Long piers ran out over the flats where now solid blocks of lofty buildings have stood for half a score of years. Sometimes storms kept back the clippers; then prices went still higher. Between March and November, flour went up from eight to forty dollars a barrel, while the "Alta" came down from its usual broad and sightly page to the size of a pane of window-glass, fourteen by ten. Villainy flourished; drinking, gambling, robbery and murder held high carnival; the law did little, and did that little shabbily and tardily; so the people woke and resumed their original legislative, judicial, and especially their executive, functions.

In '51 and '52, and again in '56, they came nobly to the front, hung the worst villains who defied the common law, frightened away the others, restored order, established security for honest men, and resolved themselves again into law-abiding citizens. And thus, through perils of fire, social convulsions, and financial fluctuation, the cosmopolitan city has swept swiftly on until to-day, though having barely attained her majority, she stands in the first half-score of American cities. Every year she leaves a city or two behind in her steady progress toward the throne of the continent which she will surely occupy before the present century has fully fled.

Situation and Extent.

In extent, population, commerce, wealth and the growth, San Francisco of to-day is not only the chief city of California, but the great commercial metropolis of the whole Pacific slope. It is both a city and a county; the county occupies the extreme end of a hilly peninsula stretching north to the Golden Gate, between the Pacific Ocean on the west, and San Francisco bay on the east.

The whole peninsula has a length of from thirty-five to forty miles, with an average width of from twelve to fifteen miles. The average width of the county from bay to ocean is four and one half miles, and its extreme length, from the Golden Gate on the north, to the San Mateo County line on the south, is six miles and a half. Its boundary line being the natural one of a coast or shore on the west, north and east, is more or less irregular; on the south it is straight. Its entire area is 26,681 acres, including the Presidio reservation of 1,500 acres, which belongs to the general government.

The county also includes the Farallon Islands, lying nearly thirty miles west in the Pacific Ocean, with the islands of Alcatraz and Yerba Buena, or Goat Island, in San Francisco bay.

The city proper occupies the northeast corner of the county. Its limits extend about two miles and a half from east to west, by three and a half from north to south, thus including between one fifth and one sixth the area of the county.

The natural surface was very uneven and the soil equally varied—sand beach, salt marsh, mud flats, low plains, narrow ravines, small and shallow valleys, elevated benches or plateaux, sandy knolls and dunes, and stretches of the close, adobe soil, made up its original surface; while rocky bluffs fortified its shore line, and extensive ledges underlaid its hills or cropped out from their sides, or crowned their tops. These hills varied in height from two hundred and sixty to four hundred and ten feet, while west and south of the city limits they rose still higher. One or two small lagoons lay sluggishly about, and as many small streams found their way thence to the bay.

The original founders of the city, as is usual in similar cases, seemed never to suspect that they were moulding the beginnings of a grand metropolis. Hence they laid out what little they did project with the least possible regard to present symmetry, or the probable demands of future growth. The natural inequalities of surface, the grade and width of streets which must become necessary to a large city, reservations for public buildings, promenades, gardens, parks, etc., with the sanitary necessity of thorough drainage, were matters of which they seem to have been serenely unconscious, or, worse still, sublimely indifferent. And many of their immediate successors in authority were legitimate descendants, or humbly imitative followers.

We have not an important street in the city which conforms its course to the cardinal points of the compass, and but one main avenue, Market street, which begins to be wide enough. As Cronise truthfully says: "The whole town stands *askew*."

We now proceed to "orient" the tourist, as Horace Mann used to say, in regard to such streets, avenues, thoroughfares, cuts, parks, etc., as mainly constitute the highly artificial, though not particularly ornamental, topography of our little occidental village.

General Plan.

Market street is the widest and the longest, starting at the water front, half a mile east of the old City Hall, and slightly ascending through eight or nine blocks, it runs thence southwesterly on a nearly level grade beyond the city limits. Its western end is yet unfinished. A mile and a half from the water it cuts through a moderately high and immoderately rocky hill, beyond which it stretches away toward the unfenced freedom of the higher hills, and the dead level of the western beach beyond, at which it will probably condescend ultimately to stop. Its surface presents every variety of natural conformation ingeniously varied with artificial distortion. Plank, rubble, McAdam, cobble, Nicolson, gravel, Stow foundation, gravel, adobe, sand, and finally undisguised dirt, offer their pleasing variety to the exploring eye. From two to four horse-railroad tracks diversify its surface with their restful regularity, while the steam cars from San José follow their locomotive a short distance up its western end.

Stately blocks, grand hotels, massive stores, lofty factories, tumble-down shanties, unoccupied lots and vacant sand-hills form its picturesque boundary on either hand. When the high summer winds sweep easterly down its broad avenue, laden with clouds of flying sand from vacant lots along its either margin, it becomes a decidedly open question whether the lots aforesaid really belong in the department of real estate, or should, properly enter the catalogue of "movable property."

We have dwelt thus at length upon this street, not only on account of its central position and superior dimensions, but because it is a representative street. Others are like it as far as they can be. They would resemble it still more closely, did length, width and direction permit. It is fast becoming the great business street of the city, and, spite of the roughness and crudeness necessarily attaching to all the streets of a new and fast-growing city, it unmistakably possesses all the requisites of the future "Grand Avenue" of the Pacific metropolis.

On the northeast of Market street, through the older portion of the city, the streets run at right angles with each other, though neither at right angles or parallel with Market. One set runs, in straight lines, nearly north and south. The other set, also straight, crosses the former at right angles, that is, running nearly east and west. The principal of these streets, as one goes from the bay westerly, back toward the hills, and, in fact, some distance up their slopes, are Front, Battery, Sansome, Montgomery, Kearny, Dupont, Stockton, Powell, Mason, Taylor, and a dozen others, of which those nearer the bay are gradually growing into importance as business streets, especially along the more level portions of their southern blocks, near where they run into Market street. Beyond these, that is, west of them, the streets are chiefly occupied by dwelling houses, among which are many expensive residences of the most modern construction and elegant design.

Between Front street and the bay run two shorter streets, Davis and Drumm, along which, as well as upon the northern part of Front street, are several of the principal wharves, piers, docks and steamboat landings.

At right angles with these streets, running back at an acute angle from Market street, and at a right angle with the water front as well as the streets already named, are Geary, Post, Sutter, Bush, Pine, California, Sacramento, Clay, Washington, Jackson, Pacific, Broadway, with a dozen or more others still further north, and a score or so south.

Along the eastern blocks of these streets, that is, within five or six squares of the water, stand many of the leading business houses, hotels, newspaper offices, etc.

A sufficient variety of pavement diversifies the surface of all these streets—from the primitive, original and everlasting cobble, destroyer of quiet, destruction to wheels and death on horses, to the smooth-rolling Nicolson and the beautifully level Stow foundation, blessed bane of all the above abominations, and not a specially bad thing for the contractors. The sidewalks generally have a liberal breadth. They are commonly covered with plank, asphaltum or brick, and, near the corners and in front of the numerous rum-holes, with gangs of bilks or crowds of loafers, who have only, as Sydney Smith once said of a certain vestry in London, to lay their heads together to make a first-class wooden pavement.

South of Market street, that is, in the newer and more rapidly growing portion of the city, the streets were laid out under a new survey, and, of course, have an angle and direction of their own. One set runs parallel with Market, that is, nearly southwest and northeast. Their names, in receding order from Market, are Mission, Howard, Folsom, Harrison, Bryant, Brannan, etc. These streets are generally wider than those of the older, northern part. Southeast of them are seven or eight parallel streets, gradually growing shorter as they come nearer the Mission Bay, ending in South street, less than a block and a half long, lying along the water front. The lower or eastern ends of nearly all these streets run down to piers and wharves, upon which are the leading lumber and coal yards of the city, the largest hay and grain barns and sheds, and the immense docks of the great Pacific Mail Steamship Company. Nearly two miles back from the water front all these streets "swing around the circle" far enough to bring them into an exactly north and south line, and creep southward down the peninsula, a block or two farther south every season.

The streets running at right angles with Market street, beginning at the water front and reckoning back southwesterly, are named by their numbers, First, Second, etc., up to Thirtieth, and even beyond. Between First street and the present water front, some six or seven blocks have been filled in and are occupied chiefly by gas works, lumber yards and large manufactories. The new streets thus formed are named, in receding order from First street, Fremont, Beale, Main, Spear, Stuart and East. To reduce blocks to miles, one has only to know that in the older part of the city the blocks, reckoning east and west, number twelve to the mile, including the streets between. From north to south they are shorter, numbering sixteen to the mile. South of Market street the blocks are about one seventh of a mile long from east to west, and one ninth of a mile wide. In both the older and newer parts of the city, the regular standard blocks are frequently subdivided by one, and sometimes two, smaller streets, running through them each way. Near the city front, the first six blocks, reckoning back from the water, have from one half to two thirds the standard size. Bearing these dimensions in mind, one can readily reduce blocks to miles, and calculate distance and time accordingly.

Approaches to the City.

From only one direction can the traveler approach the city by land; that is, by coming up from the south, through San José and the intervening places. From every other direction one approaches by water. Between Sacramento and San Francisco there are two principal routes by rail. The first brings the tourist to Vallejo, sixty miles, and thence twenty-three miles by boat, making a total of eighty-three miles, over the shortest and quickest route. Time, four hours and a half, fare, $3.00.

Approaching by this route, he comes down upon the city from the northeast. On the left, the San Pablo, Berkeley, Oakland and Alameda shores, rising gently back into broad plains, whose further edges fringe the feet of the back-lying hills. Beyond the hills, Mount Diablo. On the larboard bow, as the sailors say, that is, a little southwest, rises Goat Island, or Yerba Buena, three hundred and forty feet. This island looks "very like a whale," and in outline seems a very monster among leviathans at that.

Directly south the waters of the bay stretch so far that one can seldom discern the shore line, and may easily fancy himself looking out to sea in that direction. Further round to the right, that is, more westerly, he may catch a glimpse of Hunter's Point with the chimney and engine house of the Dry Dock. Nearer lies the Potrero, with the suburban city fast creeping up the sides, and crowning the summit of its rocky promontory. From the beach, at its nearest base, stretch out the piers and rise the grimy buildings of the Pacific Rolling Mills. Still nearer you see the south end of the long bridge, stretching southerly across Mission Bay, and connecting the Potrero with the city. In a line with the further end of this bridge, and a mile or more nearer, we have the piers and sheds of the Pacific Mail Steamship Company, with the immense ships of their China line, the largest wooden vessels afloat. The steep slope just to the right of them, on which you see the upper stories of a large brick building, is Rincon Hill, and the building is the U.S. Marine Hospital. That monument, as it seems, is the Shot Tower, while in front of, around and beyond it, you see the usual medley of ordinary city buildings, here and there rising into single or double church spires, broken by the bulk of some big business block, and relieved by the regular lines of intersecting streets.

Right of Rincon Hill, where the city fills a broad hollow, you are looking over what was once the "Happy Valley" of early times. In a line beyond it lies the Mission, which you cannot now discover, backed by the "Twin Peaks," and the high hills which form the back-bone of the peninsula. Still following around, the larger buildings of the older city meet the eye, gradually rising up the southern slope. Those singular minarets or mosque-like twin towers or spires, surmount the Jewish Synagogue. Here and there a church spire shoots above the roofs, but one sees fewer of them than in eastern cities of equal size, because the possibility of earthquakes, and the certainty of high winds, restrain architects and builders from attempting anything too lofty or exposed. Several of the finest churches in the city, spread out on the earth much more than they rise toward heaven. One reason may be that they do not own far in the latter direction.

North of the Synagogue towers, the hill still rises through three blocks, when it reaches its full height in California street hill. Then a slight depression in the hill-top outline, followed by another rise into the Clay street and Washington street hill, two blocks north and three blocks west of the former.

The higher hill still further north but nearer the front, is the famous land-mark and signal-station,

Telegraph Hill, from whose top the long familiar observatory has but recently disappeared; prostrated on a stormy night last winter, by one of the giant winds whose fury it had so long defied.

Beyond, or to the right of Telegraph hill, the city falls away to the northwest, and the bay shore also trends in that direction. Black Point, the Presidio, and finally Fort Point, bring us to the Golden Gate.

> Unfolding to empire its way,
>   Wide opened by gold and by fate,
> Swung by tides which no nation can stay,
>   Here standeth the continent's gate.

Through the narrow Gate one has a single glimpse of the grand old sea, which stretches so peacefully away under the sunset. For northern gate-post you have Lime Point; and thence the vision rests on high hills packed in behind, and gradually lifting the gaze to Mount Tamalpais, beyond whose sharply-cut summit, nothing of note attracts the sight. Between us and Tamalpais, four miles nearer and half a mile lower, close at the water's edge, we have the small but beautifully situated town of Saucelito, with its sheltered picnic grounds and tranquil bay. Beyond the Saucelito bay you can almost see through Raccoon Strait, and discover that the higher land nearer the boat is not a point, but an island. Its name is Angel Island. It is the largest and most valuable island in the bay. The Government owns it and occupies its southwestern side with barracks, garrison and parade grounds. Several batteries dot the shore at different points, and a military road around the island, connects them with the garrison.

This other small island of solid rock, crowned with a heavy fortress and girt with forts and batteries, is Alcatraz, the Pacific Gibraltar.

Instead of coming by way of Vallejo, the passenger from Sacramento may come by rail through Stockton, forty-eight miles; thence by rail to Oakland, eighty-six miles; and thence by boat to San Francisco, four miles; making a total distance of one hundred and thirty-eight miles, all rail except the last four. Through fare, $2.50.

By this route you approach the city on the east, and have only to change the point of sight from northeast to east, and remember that Goat Island will be seen close by on the right hand, that is, north of the boat, to make the description of the approach from Vallejo almost equally accurate and easily adaptable for the approach from Oakland, which is the direction from which the great majority approach.

Those who may prefer can have their choice of a third way from Sacramento, and a second from Stockton; that is by steamer, usually leaving each of those cities at noon, and due in San Francisco in eight hours. From Sacramento by water the distance is one hundred and twenty-five miles, and the fare, $1.50; from Stockton, one hundred and twenty miles, fare, $1.50; dinner on board, $1.00; staterooms, $2.00, single berths, $1.00. These boats reach San Francisco so early one seldom needs a stateroom, except in case of illness, or a strong desire for seclusion. Both lines of steamers land at the same pier, at the foot of Broadway, from ten to twelve blocks from the leading first-class hotels.

The only important route of approaching San Francisco, and riding into the city by land, lies on the south, coming from Gilroy, San José, Santa Clara, Redwood City, and intermediate places, in the cars of the Southern Pacific railroad. Coming in by this route, one traverses the fertile plains of the Santa Clara Valley, and skirts the foot-hills lying along the western base of the almost mountains, which form the divide between the bay slope and the ocean slope of the broad peninsula. Near Redwood City, and for the succeeding fifteen miles, the track runs between fresh water fields on the west and salt water marsh upon the east. From the Twelve-Mile Farm in, we strike nearer the centre of the constantly narrowing peninsula, and near San Miguel catch the first glimpse of the broad Pacific. The large building just west of the track is the Industrial School, our California House of Reformation. The southern suburbs of the city, through which we enter, present nothing remarkable beyond the usual medley of old shanties, broad vegetable gardens, pleasant, home-like cottages, and here and there the more pretentious suburban residence, increasing in number as we come nearer the centre.

We come in by Valencia street, and reach the station upon Market, just east of its junction with Valencia.

Ocean Approach.

Besides the approaches already mentioned, one may come in from Panama, Mexico, Oregon, the Sandwich Islands, Australia, Japan or China. From whichever he may come, for the last ten miles before reaching the dock, his track will be the same. A few miles west of Fort Point, all these various ocean routes converge into one, enter San Francisco Bay by the Golden Gate, and bear away southward until they intersect, and for a short distance coincide with, the approach from Vallejo, already briefly described.

Conveyances.

HACKS.—Approaching the wharf or the railroad station, you encounter the usual jargon of hotel and baggage runners, each shouting his hotel, hack or coach, as if strength of lungs was his chief stock in trade. It is but simple justice to San Francisco hackmen, however, to say that a more obliging, prompt, and courteous set, can hardly be found in any American city of equal size. That travelers may exactly understand for themselves the law regulating hacks and coaches, we quote order No. 718, of the Board of Supervisors of the city and county of San Francisco :

Section 7. "For a hackney carriage drawn by more than one horse, for one person, not exceeding one mile, $1.50, and for *more* than one person, not exceeding one mile, $2.50 ; and for each additional mile, for *each* passenger, 50 cents. For a hackney carriage drawn by one horse, for one person, not exceeding one mile, $1.00 ; for more than one person, not exceeding one mile, $1.50 ; for each passenger, for each additional mile, 25 cents."

Sec. 8. "From any landing of any steamboat, to any point east of the west line of Larkin street, and north of the south line of Brannan street, and east of Third street, shall, in all cases, be estimated not to exceed one mile."

In forty-nine cases out of fifty, no newly-arrived gentleman or lady will have any personal need to know the law; the foregoing is written mainly for the fiftieth. Bear in mind that these rates, like all fares and charges in the Golden State, are payable in gold or its equivalent coin; also, that they are the *highest*. Hackmen often carry for less.

Coaches.—Besides the hacks, one may find hotel coaches, which carry free to the hotel for which they run, or charge fifty cents for each passenger within the limits above specified.

CARS.—The red cars of the City Front line pass the head of the dock every five minutes. These carry one to the very door of the "Cosmopolitan," and "Occidental" Hotels, within one block of the "Lick House," and two blocks of the "Grand Hotel." Directly across the street from the pier of the Sacramento and Stockton steamers, half a block from the landing for passengers by rail, and one block from the landing of those coming by Vallejo, the green cars of the Sutter street line carry one directly by the "Cosmopolitan," the "Lick House," and the "Occidental," and within half a block of the "Grand." On both these lines the rate is ten cents coin for a single fare, or twenty-five cents for a coupon ticket good for four rides.

WAGONS.—At or near any landing, one can always find numbered express wagons, waiting to carry baggage for from 50 cents to $1.00, according to bulk, weight, or distance.

PORTERS.—Black, white and yellow, will serve you for "two bits," that is 25 cents, for carrying any reasonable package within reasonable distance. It is well, however, to keep your eye on porter and package.

BAGGAGE AND PACKAGE EXPRESSES.—Half an hour or more before reaching the city, either by car or boat, agents of the above companies will take your checks and your money, give you a receipt for both, and deliver your baggage, for 25 cents for each ordinary-sized trunk or valise, at any place within the single-fare limits already given. These are reliable and responsible companies, whose agents none need fear to trust. They deliver baggage promptly and in as good condition as received.

Hotels.

The foreign tourist can witness to the great lack of really fine hotels abroad. All England hardly furnishes a single hotel to rank with the best of our second-class hotels in America. Outside of Boston, New York, Philadelphia, Chicago, St. Louis, and Cincinnati, few, even of the northern cities, present any notable hotel attractions to the temporary guest. New Orleans has a single good hotel, but hardly one of the other southern cities has yet outgrown the old-fashioned "tavern."

In respect to these—in good hotels—by the immediate and unanimous verdict of every tourist, San Francisco stands preëminent. Nowhere on the continent can the traveler find beds, tables and rooms superior to those of the "Grand," the "Occidental," the "Cosmopolitan," and the "Lick House." and in no large city of America will he find as reasonable charges, considering the amount and quality of accommodation and the style of service rendered.

The usual standard rate at the four leading first-class houses, is $3.00 a day, for board and room. At the "Brooklyn," "Russ," and "American Exchange," the rates are $2.00 to $2.50 a day, for good rooms and equally good board.

THE GRAND HOTEL.—This magnificent hotel is the newest of all. It stands on the south side of Market street, occupying the whole block from New Montgomery to Second street, and stretching southward along new Montgomery, across Stevenson street to Jessie. Its north front is 205 feet, its west front 335 feet, thus covering over one acre and a half of ground. Its height is three stories, surmounted by a Mansard roof, containing a fourth. Its style of architecture may be called the "modern combination," highly ornamented. In method of construction, it is a complete frame building, surrounded by brick walls of unusual thickness. Its four hundred rooms include chambers, parlors and suits of the amplest dimensions and the richest furnishing. The halls, corridors and stairways are spacious and airy. Through all the halls, at intervals of every few feet, hang coils of fire-hose, each attached to full hydrants, and always ready for instant use. Bath-rooms and toilets abound. Barber-shop, billiard room, and the most elegantly frescoed bar-room upon the coast, occupy the most convenient portions of the basement and first floor. An amply-supplied reading-room, with most luxurious chairs, invites and detains all weary guests. Branch offices of the leading telegraphs, postal delivery box, and all needed facilities for correspondence, are at hand. Hacks stand constantly at the three spacious entrances, and four leading lines of horse-cars radiate thence to every portion of the city and suburbs.

The dining-hall accommodates three hundred. Its tables are of moderate size, surrounded by plenty of room, loaded with abundant "substantials," flanked with all the latest delicacies, and served in the most attentive manner. Breakfast rooms for private parties, and separate eating-rooms for servants and children, immediately adjoin the main dining-hall. A large and well-appointed laundry promptly accommodates guests.

If there's anything else imaginable in the whole list of first-class hotel accommodations, just mention it to your obliging host Johnson, or his courteous and efficient adjutant, Ridgeway, and it shall go hard but they will furnish it for you at once, if it is to be had within the limits of telegraph and express.

THE OCCIDENTAL.—This popular standard house stands upon the east side of Montgomery; its west front occupies the whole block from Bush street to Sutter; stretches its north flank half a block down Bush street, while its south flank goes a hundred and sixty-seven feet down Sutter street. Vertically it rises six stories into the sunshine. Four hundred and twelve elegant single and double rooms, with numerous suits having ample bathing and other accommodations, besides ladies' parlors, dining-halls, billiard-hall, convenient offices, broad stairways, spacious halls, and roomy passages, make up this truly magnificent mammoth establishment. The carpets and furniture are of the most elegant and costly description. A large and beautifully-fitted patent safety elevator adjoins the grand staircase near the main hall, and reading-room at the Montgomery street entrance.

Near the main entrance is a telegraph-office— hacks stand always in front, and four leading lines of horse-cars pass the three entrances. A newspaper and periodical stand, with post-office letter-box, complete the conveniences of the reading-room.

The walls are braced with iron, and securely anchored, besides being connected across the building by heavy iron ties on every story. Manager, Philip McShane.

COSMOPOLITAN HOTEL.—This worthy compeer of the two already described, occupies the southwest corner of Bush and Sansome streets. Centrally-located, elegantly-constructed, conveniently-arranged, and well-furnished, this house is one of the largest and newest first-class hotels. An extensive addition, including some scores of single and double rooms, richly furnished in the most modern style, sufficiently indicate its prosperity. Tubbs & Patten, managers.

LICK HOUSE.—West side of Montgomery, between Sutter and Post streets. Its east front occupies the entire block between these two streets, and runs up between one and two hundred feet of each of them. Whilst this house is excellently finished and furnished throughout, it is especially celebrated for its elegant dining-hall, which is probably more artistically-planned and exquisitely-finished than any public dining-hall in the world. Jno. M. Lawlor & Co., managers.

BROOKLYN HOTEL.—Next to the elegant hotels already named, one may reckon the "Brooklyn"—on Bush street, north side, between Montgomery and Sansome. This excellent house makes a specialty of accommodating families, having an unusually large number of suits of rooms especially designed for their comfort. Its rates are about two thirds of those before mentioned. Hotel coaches convey all guests to the house free of charge. Messrs. Kelly & Wood, proprietors.

Besides the "Brooklyn," the traveler not wishing to stop at any of the grander and dearer houses, may have his choice of the "Russ House," west side of Montgomery, from Sutter to Pine, Messrs. Pearson & Seymour, proprietors; the "American Exchange," Sansome street, west side, corner of Halleck, Timothy Sargent, proprietor; the "Morton House," formerly Orleans Hotel, 117 Post street, south side, just above Kearny; and the "International Hotel," Weygant & Partridge, 530-534 Jackson street, north side, just below Kearny.

EUROPEAN PLAN.—One fond of this style, may suit himself at Gailhard's Hotel, Nos. 507 and 509 Pine street, Pereira & Co., proprietors. "What Cheer House"—This famous hotel combines the lodging-house and restaurant under one roof, with a success of which no old Californian needs be told. Besides the usual reading-room, it has also an extensive library and museum, free to all guests; R. B. Woodward, proprietor, 525-529 Sacramento street.

Lodging Houses.

Among these we name the "Nucleus" and the "Clarendon" as equal to the best. The "Nucleus" stands on the southeast corner of Third and Market streets; David Stern, proprietor. The "Clarendon House," John M. Ward, manager, 574 Folsom street, northwest corner of Second, is new and central.

Restaurants.

Whether a man eats to live or lives to eat, he can readily suit himself here. At present rates, the traveler can get better food, greater variety, and more of it for the same money, than in any eastern city. Among the best restaurants, are Saulmann's, 520 California street, north side, between Montgomery and Kearny; Swain's Family Bakery and Restaurant, 636 Market, north side, between Montgomery and Kearny; Martin's, Commercial street; Job's, 327 Kearny; and Lermitte's Coffee Saloon, 530 Merchant street.

Baths.

The hotels usually furnish first-class facilities without the trouble of going out from under the roof. Should anyone, however, wish a more extended application of fresh or salt water, hot or cold, vapor or steam, Turkish, Russian or Roman, he has come to the very place where they have them even better than in their original countries. If you doubt it, ask Bayard Taylor.

Zeile's Baths, at 527 Pacific street, north side, between Montgomery and Kearny, furnish more natural facilities and improved artificial appliances for the scientific application of Russian, Turkish, and Roman baths, than any other establishment in Europe or America. The visitor will be surprised at the extent and completeness of every appointment in Dr. Zeile's establishment.

Places of Amusement.

No matter how busy you may be at home, you are *here* for enjoyment. When evening comes you want a good lecture, concert or play. We have them all—the first occasionally, the last two regularly. The newest, largest and finest play house is the

CALIFORNIA THEATER, on the north side of Bush street between Kearny and Dupont: John McCullough, lessee and manager. If there's a good play in the city, we generally find it here; if there are comfortable chairs and luxurious boxes anywhere, they are certainly here; and if there's an artist of good taste and a successful manager combined in one man, his name is John McCullough. The theater is new and spacious, having comfortable seats for over three thousand, one of the largest stages in the United States, with complete mechanical appliances, and finely-painted scenery and drop-curtain.

METROPOLITAN THEATER.—Montgomery street, north side, between Washington and Jackson. Occasionally occupied for transient engagements, often presenting excellent plays. Has fine acoustic properties; seats two thousand.

ALHAMBRA, 325 Bush street. This is a snug and tasty combination of theater, minstrels and opera house, usually presenting some popular and spicy blending of wit, art and song.

MAGUIRE'S OPERA HOUSE.—Washington street, north side, between Montgomery and Kearny; Thomas Maguire, proprietor. This is the famous old theater in which Forrest, Kean and Booth delighted the California audiences of earlier days.

CHINESE THEATER.—At No. 630 Jackson street the curious visitor may witness the most curious medley ever put upon a stage and called a play. An interminable and unintelligible jargon of ding-dong, clatter-clattter, tum-tum and rattle-rattle-rattle combined with falsetto screeches, wonderful gymnastics, graceful contortions, terrific sword combats, and strange old oriental masqueradings, is what you may see in the celestial play house. Half an hour of it will fully satisfy you; but every eastern visitor must needs endure at least so much.

Museums — Woodward's.— At Woodward's Gardens, Mission street, between Thirteenth and Fourteenth. This contains over ten thousand specimens of zoology, ornithology, Indian relics, alcoholic collections, natural curiosities, ancient coins, etc., besides a beautifully arranged and finely lighted art gallery, including several rare old pictures, and a sort of floral museum in the shape of a charming conservatory, wherein fragrance vies with beauty to delight and detain.

Melodeons, Dance Halls, Beer Cellars.—We hardly anticipate that the average tourist will care to be "guided" into places under this heading, but the philosophic student of human nature, as well as the curious observer of social customs, cannot consider his knowledge of any city complete until he has personally seen and actually known, not only the highest, but the lowest, amusements extensively patronized by its people. Like all other large cities, San Francisco has its share of low haunts in which really modest, and sometimes meritorious, performances blend with a much larger proportion of immodest, meretricious and disgraceful ones.

Halls.

PLATT'S HALL.—216 Montgomery, east side, just north of Bush street, is one of the most popular in the city. Popular concerts, literary lectures, religious anniversaries, educational celebrations, magical entertainments, military balls and social dances, succeed each other so rapidly that there are few nights, especially in the pleasure season, when Platt's Hall does not offer something worth going to see. Henry B. Platt, proprietor.

UNION HALL.—South side of Howard, near Third. This is the largest permanent hall in the city, and a grand place for unusually large social parties, exhibitions, political conventions and popular mass meetings. It easily accommodates upwards of three thousand.

PACIFIC HALL.—In the California Theater building, north side of Bush, just above Kearny. This is a centrally-located, tastefully-finished double hall, that is, two connected so as to be used singly or jointly according to need. Capacity, fifteen hundred.

MERCANTILE LIBRARY HALL.—In the basement of the Mercantile Library Association Building, north side of Bush street, between Montgomery and Sansome. Elegantly finished in pure white, with paneled and ornamented walls and ceilings. Accommodates eight hundred. The closeness of the neighboring buildings gives it a bad light by day, but no hall in the city lights up more brilliantly at night.

MECHANICS' INSTITUTE HALL. -- Upon the lower floor of the building of that association, south side of Post street, between Montgomery and Kearny. This is another newly-constructed, conveniently-planned, well-furnished and centrally-located hall, with a medium capacity of about six hundred.

Y. M. C. A. HALL.—Young Men's Christian Association building, north side of Sutter, just west of Kearny. A remarkably neat, well-proportioned, lofty and well-ventilated hall, having its capacity largely increased by a conveniently-sloping gallery stretching across the whole of one side, and throwing forward its flanks at either end. Capacity, six hundred and fifty.

DASHAWAY HALL.—Dashaway Society's building, south side of Post, between Kearny and Dupont. This singular name belongs to the pioneer temperance organization of the Pacific coast. Its origin can hardly be better stated than in the brief sentences of Tuthill, in his History of California: "A company of firemen, Howard No. 3, sitting in their engine house late at night, January 1st, 1859, celebrating New Year's after the custom of the country, fell to musing over their future prospects, and were vouchsafed a vision of their probable fate. At last they solemnly agreed to discontinue the use of intoxicating liquor, or, as they phrased it, to " *dash away* the cup." They accordingly organized a temperance society of " Dashaways," with Frank E. R. Whitney, chief engineer of the fire department of San Francisco, as their first President, pledging themselves to drink nothing intoxicating for five and one half months. They kept their promise, and liked it so well that, before reaching the limit of their self-imposed pledge, they renewed it for all time." Thus began the first temperance society of California, which has enrolled thousands of names, erected a fine building, founded a large library, and maintains weekly lectures to this day. In a country where wine is fast becoming a chief production, and whose greatest present danger is the social glass, the origin, efforts and success of the pioneer temperance organization merit more than passing notice.

BILLIARDS.—Tournaments and champions of this king of in-door games compel brief mention of this popular amusement and the places where one may best enjoy it. Every leading hotel has a fine billiard room attached; those of the four first named are palatial in the elegance and richness of their finish and furniture.

BOWLING SALOONS AND SHOOTING GALLERIES.—We

set these together, not because of any particular affinity between the two, but because the city has hardly enough of either to make an item of one alone. At the southwest corner of Montgomery and Pine, the enthusiastic bowler may probably find as many pins as he can prostrate, with attendants who can set them up as fast as he can knock them down; while at 913 Kearny street, he can keep up his practice, if already an expert, or "get his hand in," if a novice, at

"Shooting folly as she flies."

Those wishing the longer range for rifle practice, find it at Hermann's, near the Presidio, that is, on one's way to Fort Point.

Gymnasiums.

Although nominally a christian land, California has yet many sturdy "musclemen" within her borders, while her larger cities have several schools of various kinds, for the training of young disciples in "muscular christianity.

Chief among these in San Francisco, stands the Olympic Club, the largest physical culture club in the State. Founded in 1860, during its eleven years of ceaseless and increasing activity, over five thousand persons have availed themselves of its admirable facilities for acquiring or perfecting one's ability to "travel on his muscle." It is by no means an association of boys, or of young men only; some of the best known gray-beard pioneers, with many of the leading merchants and professional men, have enthusiastically enjoyed their daily "play-spell" within its walls for many years, and they do it still. At 35 Sutter street, south side, just below Montgomery, one may find their spacious and lofty hall, amply supplied with all the paraphernalia of modern gymnastics, and adorned with several large paintings in oil, by prominent artists who are also Olympics, besides the photographs of past and present leading members.

The San Francisco Turn-verein have their hall and rooms on the north side of O'Farrell, between Mason and Taylor. Organized in 1852, it is the oldest association in the State, owns its premises, and has an actual present membership of nearly six hundred. It is, of course, conducted upon the German plan.

Y. M. C. A.—Those who want a roll at the pins upon strictly orthodox principles, or to punch each other's heads under the sanction of christianity, can escape, or at least modify, the censure of their uncharitable spiritual superiors, by resorting to the very neat and comfortable gymnasium in the basement of the Young Men's Christian Association Building, already described. This has the great advantage and the unquestionable attraction of providing for ladies also. It has all the necessary conveniences of bath-rooms and dressing-rooms attached.

Skating Rinks.—Mercury, the fleet messenger of the gods, is fabled to have had *wings* upon his feet. Forbidden by gravity to emulate him, our modern skaters fasten *wheels* to their feet, and make up for their inability to fly by developing their power to skate. The immense floor of the Mechanics' Institute Mammoth Pavilion, on the west side of Stockton, between Post and Geary, affords the largest and smoothest rink to be found in the union. Two or three others exist in the city, besides the very large and fine new one in the pavilion at Woodward's Gardens.

Base-Ball and Cricket Grounds.—At the southeast corner of Folsom and Twenty-fifth streets, an entire block, inclosed by a high fence, leveled to the necessary smoothness and overlooked by several hundred well-sheltered spectators' seats, furnishes fine accommodations for match games of base-ball and cricket. Here the famous Red Stockings, of Cincinnati, won fresh laurels, and the officers and crew of H. B. M. ship Zealous, played the crack cricket clubs of the State.

Parks and Gardens.

WOODWARD'S GARDENS

Are on the west side of Mission street, between Thirteenth and Fourteenth. This famous resort is both park and garden, and much more besides. Its fences inclose nearly six acres, but its actual surface considerably surpasses that area, from the fact that the hill-slopes and terraces, with the various floors and galleries of the different buildings really double or even treble the original surface beneath, so that, if spread upon one level, they would cover thousands of square feet more. They thus rival any public square in size and far surpass it in variety and beauty.

We reach them, by the red cars of the City Railroad Company, leaving the west front of the Grand Hotel, at the junction of New Montgomery Avenue and Market street, every five minutes—fare five cents. Or we may go out by either the Market street, Howard street, or Folsom street cars. The first of these carry us within a little over a block of the entrance—fare, five cents; the second within a block, and the third within two blocks. Fare on the last two, ten cents for a single ride, or four tickets for a quarter. On sunny days and holiday afternoons the City Railroad runs large, open-sided excursion or picnic cars, newly constructed expressly to be run to and from the Gardens. The entrance is upon the west side of Mission, between Thirteenth and Fourteenth, through an elegant architectural gateway, or sort of façade, surmounted by four colossal statues, or carved figures. The two central figures resemble a combination of Minerva and the Goddess of Liberty; one might not go far wrong in letting them stand for

California and Oregon. The one upon either flank is a notably well-carved grizzly; larger than life and twice as natural, sitting erect upon his haunches, supporting a flag-staff with his fore paws, and with mouth slightly opened in an amiable grin of undisguised pleasure at the prominence of his elevated position, and of welcome to the visiting thousands who constantly deposit their quarters and dimes beneath his sentinel post.

Arrived within we seem to have suddenly left the windy city and dusty streets far behind. Grassy lawns surround beautiful gardens. Every variety of flowery vine and blossoming shrub alternates with rare trees interspersed here and there with artificial clumps of imported trees, or stretching along the border of the original grove native to the spot, while gravel walks wind among the whole. Immediately upon the right of the entrance, in the gate-keeper's building, is a library of nearly two thousand standard volumes, many of them rare and costly. Directly in front of the gateway, stands the

MUSEUM,

formerly Mr. Woodward's private residence — at present occupied by a miscellaneous museum of natural and artificial wonders, beasts, birds, fishes and shells, with an occasional freak of nature in the shape of a mammoth or a dwarf, or a still more startling preservation of some double-headed or six-legged specimens. The zoologist or ornithologist would scarcely get beyond this building the first day. Left of the Museum stands the

CONSERVATORY.

This is the principal one of five flower and plant houses, having an aggregate length of three hundred feet by one tenth that width. This is a really elegant crystal palace in miniature, filled with the beauty and fragrance of the rarest exotics. Through this one may pass directly to the

ART GALLERY.

The vestibule or ante-room of the Art Gallery is in fact another museum, containing two statues, an extensive collection of birds and bird's eggs; upwards of a thousand coins of all ages and nations, curious idols and weapons, with hundreds of other curiosities helpfully classified, and the whole enclosed in an ante-room elegantly proportioned and beautifully frescoed by Poldeman, in imitation of Pompeii. Thence we enter the Art Gallery proper, lighted from above—frescoed by the same artist—decorated, in the corners, with allegorical representations of Painting, Sculpture, Music and Architecture—while over the door hang the two celebrated bas-reliefs, "Night" and "Morning," by Thorwaldsen. Niches on each side contain busts of Schiller, Goethe, Tasso and Petrarch. Over sixty rare old paintings or faithful copies cover the walls.

Raphael and Salvator Rosa appear in beautiful copies; several gems from the best Dutch masters furnish a transition to the modern school, of which one or two pictures from Bierstadt, and two or three views of California scenery by Virgil Williams, stand as pleasing types.

Leaving the Art Gallery, by another exit, we stand upon the margin of a lovely little lake, around whose centre revolves the great attraction for the young folks, and no small novelty to most adult visitors, the famous

ROTARY BOAT.

This endless craft is a huge circular vessel, rigged with fore and aft sails, and seating a hundred people, who step in from the concave landing upon one side as the radial seats successively come up. It would puzzle the " cutest" old salt to find bow or stern to this curious craft; the shrewdest countrymen have to confess that they "can't make head nor tail out of the thing," while the enjoyment which the youngsters find in it, like the boat itself, never comes to an end.

Between the lake and the conservatory, an outdoor

GYMNASIUM,

with ladders, bars, rings, swings and climbing-poles, accommodates all who may wish to recreate the body. From the lake flows a little stream, along whose banks the pelican, the crane, the albatross, the wild goose and the common gull, pompously stalk or awkwardly waddle; while in its water, two or three beavers, a pair of minks and a seal or two, make their homes. Beyond this, the

HENNERY,

in which the admirer of fine poultry may see a large variety of the choicest stock. An adjoining inclosure presents a pair of ostriches, and another has two or three beautiful deer and fawn. Near the southwest corner of the garden, the

TUNNEL

carries the visitor through a heavily-timbered, securely planked, cleanly-kept and well-lighted passage under Fourteenth street, into the

ZOOLOGICAL GROUNDS

and the amphitheater. Here, ranged along the north side, backed by a high and tight fence, and fronting the south that they may have the warmest possible exposure, are the animals of the menagerie. Royal Bengal Tigers, Rocky Mountain Grizzlies, Mexican Panthers, and South American Jaguars, Australian Kangaroos, and a curious medley of dissimilar animals known as the "Happy Family," make up the caged collection. The cages are roomy, airy, cleanly and secure. The animals are remarkably fine specimens, kept in capital condition, and the keeper is intelligent and courteous.

Beyond the great cages is another range of smaller ones, containing black and cinnamon bears, foxes, badgers, raccoons, opossums, and mischievous monkeys of all sizes. Esquimaux dogs, Siberian reindeer and European elk, with many other animals, more than we have space even to catalogue, make up a collection of animated nature sufficient to stock half a dozen ordinary traveling shows, and still leave enough on hand to surpass any of them. Besides these, spacious inclosures allow Arabian and Bactrian camels a free promenade, while still beyond, another yard is tenanted by the shaggiest, sleepiest-looking, most patient and good-natured donkeys that ever allowed a gang of roistering youngsters to pack themselves upon their backs, only to be incontinently and ignominiously pitched over their heads into a promiscuous pile of dust-covered and disgusted juvenile humanity. At the extreme end of the Zoological Grounds the inclosure on the right contains a genuine Rocky Mountain Buffalo, while in the larger one upon the left, two or three reindeer contentedly browse.

AMPHITHEATER.

In the center of the zoological grounds, a large race-course, securely inclosed between inner and outer circular fences, affords free scope for Roman Chariot races, hurdle races, foot races, and equestrian performances generally. Within the inner fence, a level circle of some eighty feet diameter, accommodates acrobatic performers; while a lofty pole, rising from its center, furnishes ambitious youngsters all needed facilities for flying swings or skillful "shinning." Around this stadium are raised seats for three thousand, with a covered portion sheltering six hundred, not to mention standing room for ten thousand more.

Returning through the tunnel we turn to the left, ascend the hill and enter the

PAVILION.

This is the largest and strongest permanent wooden building upon the coast. It has the form of a parallelogram with the corners unequally cut off, thus giving its ground outline the shape of an irregular octagon. It is one hundred and fifty feet long, by one hundred and thirty wide and fifty high, surmounted by a water-tight roof, nearly an acre and a half in extent. Half a dozen broad entrances admit us to the spacious interior. Here we have a central floor; one hundred and ten feet long by ninety feet wide, as solidly laid, perfectly fitted and smoothly planed as art could make it, and furnishing the finest

SKATING RINK

imaginable, or the most capacious ball-room floor to be desired. Around this floor, a sort of dress-circle, fitted with easy seats, separated by broad aisles and roomy spaces, rises gradually back to the surrounding wall. This dress-circle accommodates three thousand spectators. Above it is a broad gallery of equal size, similarly fitted and holding as many. The gallery windows command a fine view of the underlying gardens, the meandering walks, the lake, the conservatories, shrubbery and the museum; of the zoological grounds and amphitheater further away, and of the southwestern suburbs, bounded by the Mission hills, beyond. This pavilion has a seating capacity of six thousand, while for any brief mass-meeting, four thousand more could easily stand in the nine thousand nine hundred square feet of space upon the floor. A commodious and conveniently located music, or speaker's stand, with broad stairways between dress-circle and gallery, complete the appointments of this mammoth building, whose workman-like finish and enormous strength, fully equal its huge size and immense capacity. Just west of the pavilion stands a picturesque little

TURKISH MOSQUE,

whose exterior faithfully reproduces the oriental original. Its interior is tastefully frescoed, while its domed ceiling presents an astronomical fresco, representing the starry heavens. Near the southeast corner of the pavilion is the

RESTAURANT,

so that one need not leave the grounds, should he find occasion to fill his stomach before he has sufficiently feasted his eyes. Between the restaurant and the mosque, occupying the highest point of the hill, stands

THE OBSERVATORY,

formed by a secure railing and comfortable seats inclosing and surrounding the circular top of a huge reservoir, or tank. Until the recent erection of the pavilion, this was the best point of view from which to study the plan of the grounds and enjoy their scenery; and even now, it well rewards ascent, especially for those who hardly care to climb into the pavilion gallery.

In various snug places among and under the trees, and, in some places, surrounding their trunks, are scattered scores of

LUNCH TABLES,

as a sort of out-post or picket-guard thrown out by the restaurant proper. All about the top of the pavilion hill, and for some distance down its sides, these tables, of all shapes and sizes, round, ring-shaped, triangular, octagonal, square, and "parallelogramical," and surrounded by an abundance of comfortable seats, occupy the most romantic situations. Descending the hill-slope by a winding path, we pass a broad lawn upon the left, on which the enterprising proprietor proposes the early erection of a large, conveniently-arranged fire-proof museum, for the better security of his valuable collections and cabinets.

We have now completed the general tour of this elegant park, with its delightful combination of the beautiful in nature and the wonderful in art, with the rarest curiosities of both. As a broad and airy holiday play-ground for tired pupils, as a romantic retreat for family picnics, as a pleasure-park for the quiet promenades of old and young, as a varied field of study for the naturalist, as one of the lungs through which the tired and dusty city may draw a cool, refreshing, healthful breath, and, finally, as a grand union of park, garden, conservatory, museum, gymnasium, zoological grounds and art gallery, no eastern city offers the equal of Woodward's Gardens.

City Gardens.

On the south side of Twelfth street, stretching from Folsom to Harrison, and running half a block south. Entrance on the corner of Folsom and Twelfth. Reached most directly by the Folsom street cars. Admission, 25 cts.

Menageries.

The finest in the city is that already described in the zoological department of Woodward's Gardens.

The only other is a small collection of bears, monkeys and birds at North Beach.

Squares and Parks.

The oldest and best finished public square is Portsmouth Square, commonly called the Plaza, on the west side of Kearny street, extending from Clay street to Washington street, and directly fronting the old City Hall. Besides these are Washington, Union, Columbia, Lobos, Alcatraz, Lafayette, Jefferson, Alta, Hamilton and Alamo Squares, with Yerba Buena, Buena Vista and Golden Gate Parks. The last named covers nearly 1,200 acres, (of sand at present.) Of these, the Plaza and Washington Square are the principal ones which have been sufficiently improved to merit even passing notice. To these one may add South Park, a small but elegant private inclosure occupying the centre of the block between Bryant and Brannan streets.

Promenades.

Montgomery Street.—This is the San Francisco Broadway. Flanked on either side by many of the largest and finest retail business houses, as well as two of the leading hotels. During the forenoon business monopolizes it almost exclusively; afternoons fashion claims its sidewalks, and well-nigh crowds business, not exactly to the wall, but rather upon the curbstone, if not fairly into the gutter. From three to five P. M. the tide of mammon begins to ebb, and that of fashion swells in at full flood. Fair women and frail, beauty and ugliness—calicoes, silks, satins, velvets, broadcloths, beavers and cashmere, make up the motley throng, swaying and trailing up and down the crowded thoroughfare. The faces are very fair, "as far as we can see," and the forms equally graceful, with the same limitation.

Masculine faces, broad-browed, clear-eyed, bronze-cheeked, firm-mouthed or full-bearded, impress one with the dash, the drive and the nerve which have spanned the continent with rails and bridged the Pacific with ships, ere yet the flush of full manhood has fairly settled upon them. Too many, it is true, show the full, uncertain lip, the flushed cheek and dewy eye that tell of excessive stimulus too frequently applied. Nowhere on earth is the temptation to drink stronger than here. Business is sharp, competition brisk, and the climate the most stimulating anywhere to be found. So they *drive* till nature falters or weakens and calls for rest. But rest they cannot or will not afford; the stimulus is *quicker*, it is everywhere close at hand—it seems to save time. Business men die suddenly; on the street to-day, at Laurel Hill to-morrow; heart disease, apoplexy, congestion of the lungs, or liver complaint, are among the causes most frequently assigned to the inquiring public. The causes of these causes, few stop to ask, or dare to tell.

KEARNY STREET.—Parallel with Montgomery and but a single block above, that is, west of it, runs the rival, if not already the equal, business and pleasure avenue, Kearny street. Though some single buildings on Montgomery may be finer, the average of the business blocks along Kearny street already equals, if it does not surpass that of its rival. The street itself is broader, the sidewalks wider, while the press of vehicles and the throngs of fashion are fully equal.

CALIFORNIA STREET.—At right angles with both these streets, and intersecting them near their centre, California street, the Wall street of San Francisco, runs straight down from one of the highest summits within the city limits, to within two blocks of the water front, and there debouches into Market. Its upper portion lies between elegant private residences; half way down the slope stand two of the leading city churches; below, the *Alta* office, and leading telegraph offices; thence from Montgomery down, the finest number of business blocks the city presents. On this street below Montgomery, the Bank of California, the Merchants' Exchange, the Pacific Insurance Company's Building, Hayward's, Duncan's, and Wormser's, with other blocks and buildings, present a continuous front of architectural beauty rarely equaled.

MARKET STREET.—This broad, dividing avenue which separates the older city from the newer, offers a rare architectural medley to the exploring tourist's eye. Some of the grandest business blocks on the Pacific slope tower up between or stand squarely opposite the frailest wooden shells that yet survive the "early days." Running up from the water, one encounters such noble blocks as Treadwell's, not lofty but broad, deep and strong. Harpending's whole-block front. The Grand Hotel and Nucleus foretell the size and style of the blocks which are yet to form continuous fronts along this main artery of trade.

SECOND, THIRD AND FOURTH STREETS.—South of Market, these streets come nearer to fashionable streets than any others; especially along the blocks nearer to Market. They present several single buildings of notable size and style.

THE BEST TIME.—For any walk or drive within the city limits, or on the entire San Francisco peninsular, the most comfortable hours of all the day, during the season in which the tourists commonly visit us, that is from May to September, are, unquestionably, the morning hours; the earlier the better. If you would see men and women go later; take the afternoon, face the wind and the dust, be lifted bodily off your feet, round "Cape Horn," as they call the southeast corner of Market and Third streets, until you have quite enough of that "free-soil" which may be a very fine thing in politics, but is a " beastly disagreeable thing," as our English friends might say, on a promenade.

Drives.

THE CLIFF HOUSE ROAD.—Stretches westerly from the city limits, now the west end of Bush street, to the Pacific Ocean beach—originally a mere trail over shifting sand hills. It has become the broadest, hardest, smoothest and longest track in the State. If you want an idea of California horse-flesh, and San Francisco turnouts, trot out this way almost any day. The track has a fine, hard surface wide enough, in places, for twenty teams abreast, and is often nearly filled from side to side with smooth-rolling or friendly racing teams, from the natty single buggy to the elegant coach, or the stately four-in-hand. A million dollars' worth of legs and wheels flash by a man in a very few hours on this fashionable drive, especially on a race-day. Along this road are one or two wayside inns, which, like the majority of California inns, are chiefly drinking-houses under another name. At the end stands the Cliff House, so named from its site, the solid top of a precipitous rocky bluff or cliff, overlooking the Seal Rocks, a few hundred feet west; then a thirty-mile horizon of the Pacific Ocean, broken only by the sharp rocky points of the Farallones low down under the western sky, visible only when fogs and mists and haze are wanting. Attached to the house are long horse sheds which shut off the wind from your horse while his driver goes in to interview *Foster*, mine host of the Cliff. South of the Cliff the road goes down to and out upon the Ocean House, which differs little from the popular eastern beach drives, except that it is not as wide even at the lowest of the tide, and that the ocean view thence is far more seldom diversified with sails. The beach and surf are good, however, and a brisk drive of two or three miles upon it, seldom fails to put the oxygen into the lungs—the iodine into the blood, and the exhilaration into the spirits. Some two or three miles south of the Cliff House, the road bends east, leaves the beach and starts back to the city by another way, known as the

OCEAN HOUSE ROAD, named, like the other, from the house standing near its seaward end. Approaching the city by this route, one reaches a greater height than by the Cliff House road, and when about two miles from the city, enjoys a beautiful view of the southern and western city, the shipping, the bay, the opposite shore, the trailing cities and towns, whose houses gleam between the trees of Contra Costa and Alameda counties, with their grassy foot-hills, the whole view backed and bounded by old Mt. Diablo beyond. Returning by this road, one enters the city suburbs upon the southwest by Seventeenth, or Corbett street, passes directly by the Mission with the famous old church which named it, and pursues his way back to the centre by Market, Mission, Howard or Folsom streets. Between the Cliff House and Ocean House roads, and nearer the latter, private enterprise has recently constructed a third track, known as the Central Ocean Drive.

BAY VIEW ROAD.—Drive from Market street along Third to the Long Bridge, cross that to the Potrero, keep straight on through the deep cut, over the Islais bridge, thence through South San Francisco, up a little rise, from whose summit you look down into a little valley or green bay of vegetable gardens, between which and the water stands the Bay View House, on one side of the Bay View race track. From several points as you drive out, you will readily understand why they used the phrase "Bay View" so frequently in naming localities hereabout. If you wish to return by another way, drive half a mile beyond the track, where your way runs into the older road of early times. If you have time, drive on to the brow of the hill and look down into Visitacion Valley; if not, at the acute angle where the roads become one, you turn sharply back, and after two miles of slightly uneven road, enter the city between the eastern edge of the Mission flats and the western foot of the Potrero hills.

The best time for all these drives, as already said

concerning the promenades, is morning, the earlier the better. Besides the greater purity and freshness of the air, everywhere accompanying the morning hours, one then escapes the wind and dust which, on nearly every afternoon, constitute the chief drawback from the full enjoyment of outdoor pleasure during those hours.

Libraries.

In these windy and dusty afternoons, when nature seems to frown, art and literature invite you within, and proffer quiet retreats with the best of company—good books. For a city as young and as distinctively absorbed in business, San Francisco has amply provided for the gratification of scientific research or literary taste. The chief libraries are the Mercantile, the Mechanics' Institute, the Odd Fellows', the Pioneers', and the Y. M. C. A., each of which is located in the building of the same name, presently to be noticed. Besides these, at the What Cheer House, and at Woodward's Gardens, one finds two or three thousand well selected standard volumes, free to guests and visitors.

Public Buildings.

FEDERAL.

POST-OFFICE.—The first of these to every tourist is, naturally, the Government building through which his letters come and go. This is a moderately-sized two-story building of stuccoed brick, running parallel with the west side of Battery street, between Washington and Jackson. One may enter from any street of the three. The ladies' entrance, which is also common, is from Washington street. The principal business entrance is on the west front of the building, through a cross street entered at either end from Washington or Jackson. The office opens daily at 8 A. M., and closes at 6:30 P.M., except Sundays, when its only open hour is from 9 to 10 A.M. The great overland mail for New York, by the way of Salt Lake and Omaha, closes every week day at 7:30 A. M., and on Saturdays at 3 P. M. N. B. Stone, P. M.

THE CUSTOM HOUSE is simply the upper floor of the Post-office building. Entrance on Battery, near Washington. Timothy G. Phelps, Collector.

U. S. BRANCH MINT.—The old building still occupied, and likely to be for at least a year, stands on the north side of Commercial, near Montgomery. Office hours from 9 A. M. to 2 P. M. Visitors received daily from 9 to 12. O. H. La Grange, Superintendent.

THE NEW MINT, or what is to be that building, stands on the northwest corner of Fifth and Mission streets. Its ground dimensions are $221\frac{1}{2}$ feet on Fifth, by $166\frac{1}{2}$ feet on Mission street. The basement is already built of California granite. Above the basement, which is $13\frac{3}{4}$ feet high, the walls are built of blue-gray freestone, from Newcastle Island in the Gulf of Georgia, between Vancouver's Island and the mainland of British Columbia. Thus, Uncle Sam is building his new Mint of British stone. Two stories of $18\frac{1}{2}$ feet each will surmount the high basement. The lower of these is now nearly completed. From the pavement to the crown of the roof will be 70 feet. Two chimneys will tower to the height of 150 feet.

THE U. S. MARINE HOSPITAL stands at the northeast corner of Harrison and Main streets, upon the northeast slope of Rincon Hill. This is the old building. The hospital also occupies the former buildings of the Deaf and Dumb Asylum, on the southeast corner of Mission and Fifteenth streets.

CITY AND COUNTY BUILDINGS.

OLD CITY HALL.—This famous old brick and stucco, two-story, earthquake-cracked, and iron-braced structure, with the adjoining Hall of Records, stretches along the east side of Kearny street from Merchant to Washington, and extends nearly a third of the block down each of those streets. The police-offices and lock-ups occupy the basement, while the usual District Court rooms, with Judges' Chambers and municipal offices, Supervisors' and Board of Education rooms, fill the upper floors, and clamor for more room.

THE NEW CITY HALL thus far exists only on

paper. The Commissioners have chosen an elaborate plan for a costly edifice, which will far surpass anything on the coast in architectural beauty; but the execution of that plan has hardly yet completed the excavation for the foundation walls. Hence it is yet too early to tantalize the tourist with descriptions of a beautiful building not yet visible, except in the architect's drawing, or the lithographic copies. If any tourist is curious to see the *site*, he may find it by going out Market street till he reaches what was known as Yerba Buena Park, corner of Market and Seventh streets. The City Hall Commissioners adopted the plans and specifications of Mr. Augustus Laver, of New York, and elected him architect; but, at the present rate of progress, it is hardly probable that less than two or three years will witness the completion of the urgently-needed and magnificently-designed new City Hall.

JAIL.—On the north side of Broadway, between Dupont and Kearny, one desirous of inspecting our penal institutions may find ample opportunity to study the physiognomy of that class which inhabits them, and learn the crimes which preponderate in the Pacific metropolis. Sheriff, P. J. White.

ALMSHOUSE.—This asylum occupies one of the healthiest locations in the State, near the Ocean House, or San Miguel road, about four and one quarter miles southwest of the City Hall. M. J. Keating, Superintendent.

INDUSTRIAL SCHOOL.—This finely-constructed, conveniently-arranged and well-managed reform school, stands on the western slope of the peninsula hills, about seven miles southwest of the city. Like the Almshouse it has as healthful a location as can be found in the State. It receives only boys, who are regularly taught by competent teachers, and employed in various indoor occupations or out-door work. Present number of inmates, two hundred and twelve. The order and discipline of this school well repay a visit. Jno. C. Pelton, Superintendent.

ENGINE HOUSES.—In early days, before the establishment of homes, the pioneer firemen seemed to love their machine very much as the sailor loves his ship. They built elegant and costly engine houses, which became to many of them the only homes they ever knew. Since the introduction of the improved steam fire engines, and the organization of the paid fire department, the glory of the old volunteer organizations has well nigh departed. But their houses yet remain, some of them converted to other uses, while others still retain much of their earlier attractiveness.

Eight first-class steamers, of the Amoskeag make, weighing from three to four tons each, throwing four hundred gallons a minute, each costing from four to five thousand dollars in gold coin, and manned by twelve men, make up the present paid fire department. At a public trial a week since,

New York and Philadelphia witnesses voluntarily and unanimously testified that they had never seen machines reach the spot as soon and get a stream upon the flames as quickly, as did the machines of our fire department. This fact may conduce to the sense of security with which the eastern tourist lies down to sleep in his strange bed. For the benefit of any extra nervous gentleman, we may add the universal rule of conduct in regard to midnight alarms of fire among us, is this : When waked by a fire-alarm, place your hand against the nearest wall. If it feels cold, lie still ; if moderately warm, order a different room at once ; if positively *hot*, leave for another hotel immediately.

CORPORATION AND SOCIETY BUILDINGS.

THE PIONEER'S BUILDING.—A finely proportioned building on the corner of Gold and Montgomery streets, above Jackson. This building is not as noteworthy as the society which built and chiefly occupies it. The famous " Society of California Pioneers" was formed in August, 1850. Its constitution declares its object to be:

"To cultivate the social virtues of its members ;

" To collect and preserve information connected with the early settlement of the country; and

"To perpetuate the memory of those whose sagacity, energy and love of independence induced them to settle in the wilderness and become the germs of a new State."

It includes three classes: 1st. Native Californians; foreigners living in California before the American conquest; and citizens of the United States who became actual residents here before January 1st, 1849—with the male descendants of these.

2d. Citizens of the United States who became actual residents of California before January 1st, 1850, and their male descendants.

3d. Honorary members admitted according to the by-laws. The society has enrolled over 1,300 members. Its historical library and museum well repay a visit. Charles D. Carter, President.

MERCHANT'S EXCHANGE.—This building, the commercial headquarters of the mercantile army of the Pacific, stands on the south side of California street, between Montgomery and Sansome. It ranks among the largest and finest architectural ornaments of the city.

BANK OF CALIFORNIA.—Northwest corner of California and Sansome. This elegant stone structure is not remarkable for size; but for broad and deep foundations, slow and strong construction, harmonious proportions, convenient arrangements and admirable finish within and without, it ranks among the finest and most costly business buildings in the Union. President, D. O. Mills. Cashier, William C. Ralston.

MERCANTILE LIBRARY BUILDING.—North side of Bush

street, between Montgomery and Sansome. This is the building for which the great lottery paid. It presents a noble front, a finely finished interior, with library room containing over 30,000 volumes, reading room, magazine room, reference room, chess room, with a large ladies' room of remarkably costly and tasteful furnishing. The hall in the basement, has already been noticed. Ogden Hoffman, President; Alfred Stebbins, Librarian.

MECHANICS' INSTITUTE BUILDING.—South side of Post street, just below Kearny. A well-proportioned, substantially built, sensible-looking building, and so far truthfully indicative of the healthful prosperity of the excellent organization which owns and occupies it. A library of nearly 20,000 volumes, including many rare and costly scientific works, a large and well-stocked reading room, a sort of museum, including mineralogical cabinets, mechanical models, scientific apparatus and works of art, with a popular business college, occupy this valuable building. The commodious hall upon the lower floor, has been previously described.

MECHANICS' PAVILION.—Union Square, between Geary and Post streets on the south and north, and Stockton and Powell streets on the east and west. One of the largest, if not the largest, wooden buildings now standing in America, covering two and one half acres of ground; originally erected by the Mechanics' Institute Association, for the accommodation of their biennial fairs, and found almost indispensably convenient for all grander gatherings; it has since been retained, and successively occupied by fairs, grand masquerade balls, velocipede schools and skating rinks. The most notable event occurring under its mammoth roof was the Grand Musical Festival or Gift Concert, in aid of the Mercantile Library Association, given under the lead of Madame Camilla Urso. After the approaching Mechanics' Fair, to be held this summer, the building is to be removed.

MASONIC TEMPLE.—Upon the west side of Montgomery, at the corner of Post; of peculiar and attractive architecture, imposing proportions and elegant finish, it justly ranks among the most prominent buildings of the city.

ODD FELLOWS' HALL.—Montgomery street, between Pine and California. Not particularly imposing from without, but attractive from the unity, strength and beneficence of the Order which it represents. Within are a library of nearly 20,000 standard and popular volumes, a well-supplied reading-room, and a well-managed savings' bank.

Y. M. C. A.—This quartette of initials has now become so well known throughout the larger cities of the Union, that the visitor in any large city is disappointed if he does not find the local habitation of this fast-spreading bond of unity among all good men. Here, upon Sutter street, just above Kearny, he will be agreeably disappointed to discover a large, new, stone-front building, unique in design, and most pleasing in its general effect. Within are library, reading-rooms, hall, gymnasium, and several convenient lodging-rooms. Chas. Goodall, President; H. L. Chamberlain, Librarian.

Business Buildings and Blocks.

ALTA CALIFORNIA BUILDING—On the south side of California street, between Montgomery and Kearny. Its comparatively great height, as related to its width, give it a somewhat monumental appearance, not inappropriate, however, when we remember that the whole tasteful structure stands as the monument of the enterprise, energy, perseverance and success of the oldest and largest paper published in the State. Fred. MacCrellish & Co., proprietors.

BANCROFT'S—South side of Market street, between Third and Fourth. Few business buildings upon the continent combine the colossal proportions with the graceful details of this mammoth house of the oldest and largest publishing firm upon the coast.

DONOHOE, KELLY & Co.'s BUILDING— Upon the southeast corner of Montgomery and Sacramento streets, deserves mention among the finest business buildings.

HARPENDING'S BLOCK—On the south side of Market street, between First and Second; the longest and loftiest business front presented by any single business block in the city.

Murphy, Grant & Co's. Building—Northeast corner of Bush and Sansome. A large and handsome building, as strong as iron, stone and brick can make it.

Tobin, Dixon & Davisson's Building—Northwest corner of Sansome and Sutter, can hardly be omitted from the inspection of our finest business houses.

Treadwell's Agricultural Warehouse—South side of Market street, opposite Front. Not lofty, but broad; not imposing, but extensive.

Tucker's—Northwest corner of Montgomery and Sutter. Lofty, finely-proportioned, monumental, and substantial; surmounted by a clock-tower, which has become one of the landmarks of the city. The main salesroom within is beautifully frescoed and fitted throughout with extreme elegance and at great cost.

The White House—Corner of Kearny and Post streets. An elegant new iron and brick structure, light, airy and ornamental in its general effect. Receives its name from its color, which has hitherto been an uncommon one in this city, but is daily becoming less so. Occupied chiefly by the leading dry goods firm of J. W. Davidson & Co.

Wells, Fargo & Co's. Building—Corner of California and Montgomery streets. Who does not know it? Solid granite blocks, dressed in China, brought hither in ships, and piled in stern simplicity upon that central corner to outstand all earthquake shocks, and survive all business wrecks. A pioneer building which has already become far too small for its immense business, but ought never to be taken down until the whole city goes with it.

Manufactories.

KIMBALL CAR AND CARRIAGE FACTORY.—Corner of Bryant and Fourth streets. Eastern visitors call this the largest establishment of the kind in America. In immense extent, convenient arrangement, and comprehensiveness of scope, it can hardly be surpassed. Its latest triumph is the construction of a magnificent Palace Car, built wholly of California woods, undisguised by paint, carving, gilding, or varnish—the most complete and superb palace on wheels ever built. Thirty-five different woods enter into its construction, displaying a variety of structure and a range of harmonious tints hardly imaginable by those who have seen only the poor imitations of feeble art. The car is a triumph of taste and skill, and is worth a half-day's time of any tourist simply to study and enjoy it. It has been proposed that the merchants of this city buy it, and present it to the President of the United States—to *the office*, not the *incumbent*—to be kept at Washington, and used as the official car for all

Presidential tours. A better idea could hardly be suggested. May the motion prevail!

THE PACIFIC ROLLING MILLS stand upon the point of the Potrero. They include all the massive machinery of their ponderous business, and turn out heavy castings, forgings, and railroad iron by hundreds of tons daily.

THE MISSION WOOLEN MILLS—Folsom street, corner of Sixteenth. Here are made those wonderful blankets of such marvelous fineness and thickness, which have attracted so much attention, and received even the World's Fair premium abroad.

Foundries and Iron Works.

UNION IRON WORKS.—The oldest and largest in California, employing three hundred and thirty men, and turning out the heaviest and most perfect mining and railroad machinery, locomotives, etc. Located on the northeast corner of Mission and First streets. H. J. Booth & Co.

RISDON IRON AND LOCOMOTIVE WORKS, southeast corner of Howard and Beale streets. Has all the latest mechanical improvements of the business. Can turn out a shaft forty-eight feet long, and weighing thirty tons. It employs two hundred and seventy-five hands. John N. Risdon, president.

The Fulton, Miners', and Pacific Foundries, with the Etna and Vulcan Iron Works, are the other leading ones of the coast.

Shot Tower and Lead Works.

Corner of Howard and First streets. The pioneer and, thus far, the only works upon the coast. The tower is one of the most prominent and sightly objects visible in all the water approaches to the city.

Sugar Refineries.

The city has four: The San Francisco and Pacific, Bay, California, and Golden Gate, turning out twenty thousand tons of sugar annually.

Ship Yards.

At North Beach and at the Potrero are the principal yards. They build mainly river steamers or ferry boats, or smaller ocean craft, rarely constructing anything above three hundred tons. For larger craft it is cheaper to go north, where immense forests of the finest ship-timber run clear down to the ocean beach, and stand asking to be built into ships.

Glass Works.

Two: one in the city, on the south side of Townsend, between Third and Fourth; and the other, the Pacific Glass works, on the Potrero, at the corner of Iowa and Mariposa streets. These confine their works chiefly to bottles, telegraph caps, etc.

Churches.

BAPTIST.—This prominent denomination has six

church buildings in the city. The First Baptist Church claims special space from the fact that it was the first Protestant house of worship dedicated in California. This was in August, 1849. The present building of stuccoed brick, occupies the original site of the first small, wooden pioneer church—on the north side of Washington street, between Stockton and Dupont. Rev. A. R. Medbury, Pastor.

CONGREGATIONAL.—This denomination has the honor of having furnished the first settled Protestant chaplain in San Francisco, Rev. T. Dwight Hunt. He held the rare position of "Citizens' Chaplain," Nov. 1st, 1848, conducting Divine worship every Sunday in the "Public Institute," (the school-house) on Portsmouth Square—the Plaza. The citizens unitedly invited him from Honolulu, and paid him $2,500 a year. The denomination has four church buildings--named by their order of erection. The First Congregational Church is on the southwest corner of California and Dupont streets. The pastor is Rev. Dr. Stone, formerly of the Park street church, Boston.

EPISCOPAL.—This denomination has five church buildings, of which Grace Church, corner of California and Stockton streets, is the oldest and largest. The building is 135 feet long, 62 feet wide and 66 feet high. Its great size and sightly location make it one of the prominent buildings in any general view of the city. Rev. James S. Bush, Rector. The four other Episcopal church buildings are—Trinity, St. John's, Church of the Advent, and St. Luke's.

HEBREW. — Synagogue of the Congregation Emanu-el, Sutter street, between Stockton and Powell. · Of the five Jewish congregations, this has "The Synagogue" par excellence—the one always meant when one speaks of "The Jewish Synagogue." It is an elegant and costly structure, built of brick, not yet stuccoed, supporting two prominent towers, and finished within in most appropriate and artistic style. Total cost, including lot, $185,000, gold coin.

METHODIST.—This popular, powerful and rapidly growing denomination has already erected eleven church buildings in San Francisco—more than any other Protestant Church, except the Presbyterians. Its newest and most elegant church is the First Methodist Episcopal Church, on the west side of Powell, between Washington and Jackson. This is one of the most elegant and really artistic churches, within and without, any where to be found. Rev. Dr. Cox, Pastor.

HOWARD STREET M. E. CHURCH.—South side of Howard, between Second and Third. This is the most substantial and valuable building owned by the denomination. Value, including lot and parsonage, $100,000. Its style is medieval gothic. Pastor, Rev. L. Walker.

PRESBYTERIAN.—This recently united denomination, no longer old and new school, has also eleven church buildings; of these the two most noted are the Calvary Presbyterian Church, corner of Geary and Powell streets. This church is as capacious and comfortable, even luxurious within, as the most fastidious could desire. Its organ is the largest and finest on the coast. Rev. J. Hemphill, Pastor.

Howard Presbyterian Church, Mission street, near Third; lately, Rev. Dr. Scudder's. This building, with a plain and unpretentious exterior, has greater seating capacity than any other Protestant church in the city. It is of recent construction and very convenient internal arrangements. Temporary pastor, Rev. J. K. Kendall.

First Presbyterian Church—On the west side of Stockton, between Washington and Clay. This gothic building is one of the largest and finest—but its chief claim to notice here, rests upon the fact that the church which built it, organized May 20th, 1849, under the direction of the Rev. Albert Williams, was the first Protestant church organized in San Francisco.

ROMAN CATHOLIC.—St. Patrick's Church, on the north side of Mission, between Third and Fourth streets. Although so new that it is not yet finished, this church is set first, because it is the largest in the State, being one hundred and sixty feet long by eighty feet wide. Its spire is the loftiest and most beautifully proportioned in the city, height 240 feet. Rev. Peter J. Grey, Pastor.

St. Mary's Cathedral, California street, at the northeast corner of Dupont. In age, cost and rank this building is entitled to the first place. It is a noble structure of Gothic architecture, which has been carried out in every detail. The front extends seventy-five feet on California street, from which the cathedral runs back one hundred and thirty-one feet on Dupont. The tower is at present one hundred and thirty-five feet high, and is to be surmounted by a spire rising sixty-five feet further. The Most Rev. Joseph S. Alemany is the Archbishop.

Old Mission Church, on the southwest corner of Sixteenth and Dolores streets. This was dedicated Oct. 9, 1776, by Father Junipero Serra, the father of the California missions. Aside from its age and associations, the building is of little note. It is built of the old adobes, which were simply unburnt bricks dried in the sun, and formed a favorite building material with the early Spanish and Mexican inhabitants. The old custom-house, on Portsmouth square, was built of this material. The roof was covered with semi-cylindrical tiles of burnt clay, laid in alternate rows, the first one having the concave side up, and the next its convex side up. The outside, generally, is very plain, though the front shows some old-fashioned round columns, and a few small bells suspended in square apertures under the projecting roof. The interior is dark, cold and comfortless. Rev. Thos. Cushing, Pastor.

Besides the three churches already named, the Catholics have nine others in the city, in addition to five or six chapels and asylums.

SWEDENBORGIAN.—First New Jerusalem Church. This is a very neat Gothic building, on the north side of O'Farrell, between Mason and Taylor streets. Rev. John Doughty, Pastor.

A second New Jerusalem Church, of which Rev. Joseph Worcester is pastor, having yet erected no building, meets in the Druids' Hall, No. 413 Sutter street.

UNITARIAN.—First Unitarian Church. This most beautiful church edifice stands upon the south side of Geary street, just below Stockton. Its front presents, unquestionably, the finest specimen of church architecture in the State, and can hardly be surpassed in America. The interior is tastefully decorated with a colored fresco of extreme beauty, and most artistic harmony of tint. The organ, baptismal font, and the pulpit, perpetuate the unique taste of the lamented pastor, whose loved name the public mind cannot dissociate from the beautiful building, which, always known as "Starr King's" church, has become his fitting monument.

This is the only church building of this denomination in the city or the State.

CHINESE MISSION HOUSE.—This is a combination church and school-house, new, neat and commodious, fifty-six feet by seventy feet, and three stories high. Adjoining school-rooms, readily thrown into one, rooms for the Superintendent, Rev. Mr. Gibson and family, and for his assistant, Rev. Hu Sing Me, the native preacher, and his family, occupy the various floors. School "keeps" every evening in the week, except Saturday and Sunday. Bible class at half-past ten every Sunday morning, and Sunday school at seven P. M.

The entire property belongs to the Methodist Church, who maintain it as a most efficient home mission.

The Mariner's Church, northeast corner of Sacramento and Drumm streets. It is a neat and commodious wooden building, erected in 1867, by contributions from merchants and other citizens of San Francisco. Rev. J. Rowell, Pastor.

Hospitals and Asylums.

CITY AND COUNTY HOSPITAL.—Stands upon the southwest corner of Stockton and Francisco streets.

FRENCH BENEVOLENT SOCIETY.—Has one of the finest hospitals of the State, a large and handsome brick building, surrounded with pleasant gardens and ornamented grounds, occupying the whole block on the south side of Bryant, between Fifth and Sixth, making a most agreeable and healthful home for the invalid. Others besides French may receive its benefits, by assuming membership and paying its moderate dues.

GERMAN GENERAL BENEVOLENT SOCIETY.—Admits only Germans. It has over eighteen hundred members. On Brannan street, near Third, this society has a very large two-story brick building with basement—furnished with every form of bath, and looking out upon fine gardens and shrubbery.

PROTESTANT ORPHAN ASYLUM.—On the West side of Laguna street, between Haight and Waller. A large and elegant building of brick and stone—one of the ornamental landmarks of that part of the city. It accommodates two hundred and fifty little ones. Mrs. Ira P. Rankin, President; Mrs. Lucy Stewart, Matron.

ROMAN CATHOLIC ORPHAN ASYLUM.—Market street, south side, between New Montgomery and Third. A noble and capacious brick building accommodating three hundred and twenty children, and having a school of five hundred and fifty day scholars attached. The Asylum is under the sole management of Archbishop Alemany and the Sisters of Charity.

SAN FRANCISCO FEMALE HOSPITAL.—Corner of Clay

street and Prospect Place. Any woman who is sick and poor, has a right to its benefits. It is a genuine charity, regarding neither nativity, religion nor social rank. Mrs. M. R. Roberts, President; Dr. C. T. Deane, Physician.

LADIES' PROTECTION AND RELIEF SOCIETY.—Franklin street, between Post and Geary. The main object of the society is to furnish a real *Home* for friendless or destitute girls, between three and fourteen years old. Boys, under ten and over three, may be received and provided for until furnished with a permanent home in a christian family. It has over two hundred inmates, nearly all girls. Miss C. A. Harmon, Matron.

Nearly a hundred other public and private benevolent societies attempt to make up, as well as possible, the lack of friends and homes, always so severely felt by strangers or temporary residents in any large city, and especially so in one of as cosmopolitan a character as ours.

Colleges.

Besides the larger public schools, which are really the peoples' colleges—the city has sixty-five colleges and private schools. The number of pupils attending them in 1870 was 4,582, against 21,000 in the public schools."

CITY COLLEGE.—Southeast corner of Stockton and Geary streets. This institution has built and furnished an elegant French Gothic building at University Mound, some three miles southwest of the city, which it will occupy early in '72. Besides the usual studies, this college especially provides the best facilities for obtaining a thorough practical knowledge of Chemistry, in all its applications to assaying, mining, medical manufactures and mechanics. Rev. Dr. Veeder, President.

HEALD'S BUSINESS COLLEGE.—College Building, Post street, between Montgomery and Kearny. Its design is to educate boys and young men, with a special view to practical business. It is one of the famous thirty-six Bryant and Stratton Business Colleges, located in the leading cities of the United States and Canada. Students, two hundred and fifty. E. P. Heald, President.

ST. IGNATIUS' COLLEGE.—Occupies the noble brick building on the south side of Market street, between Fourth and Fifth. It is largely attended, and is successfully conducted by the Jesuit Fathers.

ST. MARY'S COLLEGE.—On the old county road to San José, four and a half miles southwest of the city. Building, two hundred and eighty feet front, by fifty feet deep—of excellent proportion and fine appearance. Conducted by the Christian Brothers. B. Justin, President.

TOLAND MEDICAL COLLEGE.—East side of Stockton street, between Chestnut and Francisco. The building is of brick, capacious, commodious, finely located and admirably adapted to the purpose of its construction. H. H. Toland, M. D., President.

Public School Buildings.

Lincoln.—Fifth street—south side, near Market. Brick structure, four stories high, 141½ feet long, 63½ feet wide; 20 class-rooms 129x34 feet, besides eight wardrobes and teachers' rooms—wide halls, and four broad stairways the whole height, with a large hall in the upper story. It accommodates twelve hundred grammar grade pupils, all boys. In front stands a finely modeled statue of Abraham Lincoln for whom the building was named. Cost, $100,000, gold coin. B. Marks, Principal.

Denman.—Bush street, north side, corner of Taylor. Brick stuccoed; length, 98¼ feet; width, 68 feet; height, four stories, including attic rooms. Fourteen class-rooms, each 28x34, accommodating eight hundred pupils, all girls. Cost, $78,000, gold. This building was named in honor of James Denman, one of the pioneer public school teachers of the city—the founder of this school and for many years, as at present, its principal. Few cities in the Union can show school buildings as elegant, convenient, substantial and costly as these two noble monuments of public appreciation of, and liberality towards, the system which must underlie and sustain our free government if it is to stand at all.

TEHAMA.—Tehama street, near First. Brick, undisguised; 111 feet long, 75 feet deep, three stories high, besides spacious basement play-rooms—has sixteen class-rooms, each 24x31, hall, 41x49, with ample stairings, and convenient teacher's-rooms and ample yards. Cost, $28,300, gold. It accommodates one thousand primary pupils of both sexes. Mrs. E. A. Wood, Principal.

Besides these, the city has several large and fine wooden school-houses of modern structure. Of these the most sightly, is the Girls' High School, south side of Bush street, near Stockton—57x92, three stories, ten class-rooms, 27x34, with an assembly hall, 54x55; whose length can be increased to 90 feet, by opening folding doors between it and two adjoining class-rooms. It is the most conveniently arranged, best ventilated, sunniest, most cheerful and healthful school-house in the State. Ellis H. Holmes, Principal. To these the Department has recently added, and is now adding, four or five 18 class-room buildings, of wood, each accommodating one thousand pupils, now occupying the old and small school-rooms of early days or hived in unsuitable rented rooms.

Bancroft's Book and Stationery Establishment.

It may appear like exaggeration to say that San Francisco contains the largest and most complete general Book and Stationery, mercantile and manufacturing business in the world. Yet, such is the fact. Not that the business, by any means, equals that of Harpers' and Appletons', of New York, Hachette of Paris, or the stationers of London. But, between these houses and Bancroft's, there is no comparison. The character of their trade is totally different. One publishes books, another manufactures paper, and so each is large in one thing, whereas the Bancrofts, collecting from the manufacturers of all the world, and manufacturing according to the requirements of their trade, cover under one management the ground occupied by all others combined. In older and larger cities, one house deals in law books alone; another, school books, etc., while this San Francisco house—besides a full stock of books in every department of literature, and stationery from the manufacturers of Europe and America, paper from the mills of New England, pencils from Germany, pen-holders from Paris—unite Printing, Book-binding, Lithography, Blank-Book Making, Engraving, &c., every thing, in short, comprised in all the business of all the others.

The detail is necessarily very great. They buy from a thousand sellers, and sell to many thousand buyers. Over one hundred employés, divided into nine departments, each under an experienced manager, ply their vocation like bees in a hive of six rooms, each 37 by 170 feet. To the latest improvements of the finest machinery, driven by steam, apply the highest order of skilled labor, and San Francisco can do anything as well and as cheaply as New York, London or Paris.

The retail department, occupying the first floor, has the most magnificent salesroom on the Pacific coast. Visitors are warmly welcomed, and strangers politely shown through the premises.

Private Residences.

For the convenience of the tourist, who may want to see the homes of our city as well as her public buildings and business blocks, we mention the locality of the following, which are among the finest of our private dwellings: Erwin Davis, southwest corner of California and Powell streets; Milton S. Latham, Folsom street, opposite Hawthorne, on Rincon Hill; D. J. Tallant, corner of Bush and Jones street; Richard Tobin, corner of California and Taylor streets; John Parrott, 620 Folsom street. By making two trips—first, over California street, and returning by Sutter or Bush street; second, over Rincon Hill on Folsom street, and returning by Harrison, the visitor may see the finest of our private residences.

Points of Observation.

TELEGRAPH HILL.—This notable natural landmark stands at the head, that is, at the north end of

Montgomery street. The early settlement, the pioneer hamlet from which the present city has grown, was made in the hollow near the southwest foot. Civilization has encircled it on the land side, and crept two thirds the way up, while commerce has claimed the water front along its opposite base—but the summit still stands as free as when the priestly fathers first looked thence upon the glorious inland sea, which flashes between it and the sunrise. Let us climb it—this way, straight up the Montgomery street sidewalk. Slowly, please; we have the day before us; exhausted lungs impair one's sight. Stop at the corner of each intersecting street, and glance either way, but especially eastward—that is, downward toward the Bay. Now, "Excelsior," again; up these stairs; now along this natural surface—no asphaltum walks or Stow foundation pavements up here yet, you see—on, by these houses; turn to the left here; now to the right, follow this winding way; patiently please—that's it; only two or three minutes more —ah! here it is—this is the highest point, where the old observatory stood. Sit and breathe a moment; slip on your overcoat, or put that extra shawl about you; it's easy to take cold here, far easier than to rid yourself of it in the city below.

For the sake of method in our survey, we may as well begin at the northwest; thence " swing round the circle," through north, east, south and west, and return to the point of starting. Looking northwesterly, then, we have first the elevated, undulating plateau, which stretches along the flattened summits of the northernmost spur of the broad peninsular hills, and terminates in the precipitous bluff known as Fort Point—the southern gate-post of the far-famed Golden Gate. Through this we gaze seaward along the further margin of the strait, where it sends in a surging cove upon the rocky beach, between Point Diablo and Point Bonita. The projection of the latter point shuts off the vision, which else might range up the northwesterly trend of the coast, along the ocean-shore of Marin county to Punta de los Reyes, (King's Point) which projects southward between Bolinas bay and the ocean. Between Point Diablo and Lime Point, a slight northerly curve in the shore line makes a shallow cove, from whose edge the vision climbs the successive hills or ridges which fill the ascending space as it roughly rises toward the crowning point of Marin county, Mount Tamalpais, two thousand six hundred and four feet nearer heaven than the beach line whence we set forth. Still following round, we look up into Richardson's Bay; next the southwestern end of Raccoon Strait, and then Angel Island. We are now looking north. Alcatraz, the rocky island which nature set just there to support a commanding fortress; then, an eye-sweep up over the northern part of San Francisco

Bay to that narrow strait which joins it with San Pablo Bay; northeast the San Pablo shore of Contra Costa county, and the hills which terminate the Mount Diablo peninsular range. Nearer east, the strangely monotonous hills, whose ridges and gullies look as if plowed out by heavy rains, and rounded by sweeping winds. Grassy or earthy, they look, according to the time of year and kind of season. Now, almost east, the vision falls. This large island, off in the midst of the bay, is Yerba Buena, or Goat Island. It rises three hundred and forty feet above low water mark. Nearly in a line over the island appears Berkeley, the site of the University of California, of which one large building, already two thirds raised, you may possibly discern. A little further south—that is, to the right, you can plainly see the State Asylum for the Deaf and Dumb and Blind. This noble building crowns a gently-sloping eminence just at the margin between the broad and nearly level plain which stretches between it and the bay, and the foothills back of which the Contra Costa mountains bring up the rear.

Almost due east lies Oakland, the tree-city of the beautiful grove-dotted plain. Then Clinton, San Antonio, Brooklyn and Alameda, snuggled in together so closely that one can't tell " which is which;" and, as far as the beauty of the view is concerned, it doesn't matter either, for they are all fair to look upon and lovely to behold. The clustering trees shut out by far the larger portion of the houses, so that we might hardly suspect the size and population of the towns, whose scattered roofs show here and there among the trees.

We are looking southeasterly now. That creek, whose mouth you see just beyond Alameda, leads into San Leandro bay; and right over it, nearly hidden by intervening trees, lies the town of the same name. A little further south, and too distant to be plainly seen, is Hayward's. That depression in the mountain summits beyond, marks the opening of Livermore pass, through which the Western Pacific Railroad finds its way.

Beyond Hayward's, further south, and thence sweeping around to the right, toward the extreme end of the bay, we dimly discern the northern end of the beautiful Santa Clara Valley, where it widens out and flattens down to the bay. We are now looking almost due south. Only four miles down, Hunter's Point shuts off our further view, and compels us to look nearer home. A trifle west of that, and half as far away, the Potrero presents its transverse ridge, fast disappearing under the rapidly-growing city, and showing a gap of daylight where the deep cut of the Bay View horse railroad was relentlessly dug and blasted through, in its stubborn pursuit of a practicable grade. Between the cut and ourselves, the Long Bridge shuts off the Mission bay, and shows where the fast-filling mud-flats will soon crowd back the bay, and make a new water front. Still nearer, we have the western slope or ridge of Rincon Hill, rising gradually to the left, and packed all over with the huddled and mostly wooden houses of the new and hurriedly-built city. Along the inner base of the hill, and stretching out westward, lies the old "Happy Valley." That's just this side of where you see the shot-tower, and runs thence four or five blocks to the right. Between that and ourselves, coming over this side of Market street, we have the oldest and most densely-built part of the city, relieved here and there—by the Occidental Hotel, Tucker's tower, the Merchants' Exchange, Murphy, Grant & Co's. building, and half a dozen others. Now let the vision range away southwest, again beginning at the hills and coming in. The bounding hills are Bernal Heights, west of which Fairmount and the adjacent hills merge into the peninsular range, and form a rude amphitheatre, within which nestles the fast-growing southwestern precinct. Coming up toward the west, the twin summits of the Mission peaks slant the vision up against the sky, or plunge it into the fleecy billows of in-rolling ocean fog, which seldom survives the warmer air of the inner basin long enough to roll far down their western slope. Between them and us lies the Mission Dolores, grouped around its century-old church. Northward of the twin-peaks the hills rise in " promiscuous prominence." A little south of west, that irregularly conical hill, surmounted by a gigantic solitary cross, is the famous " Lone Mountain," about whose lower slopes, and around whose base are grouped so many " cities of the dead." Thence northerly, to the point whence our survey began, little of note arrests the sight, more than the broad reach of lower hills and sandy dunes, which patiently wait the coming occupation of the westward-growing city.

Although the point beneath our feet is but three hundred feet high, the panoramic view is wider and freer than from any other, even the highest hilltop of the city.

RUSSIAN HILL.—About one mile west-southwest from Telegraph Hill, on Vallejo street, between Taylor and Jones street, Russian Hill rises nearly sixty feet higher, but offers little additional prospect. It was formerly surmounted by a sort of cork-screw observatory, a skeleton structure of open frame-work, surrounded by a spiral stairway, whose summit afforded the loftiest lookout within the city limits. West-northwest of this hill, and about three-quarters of a mile from its summit, lies the small lagoon, near which the founders of the early mission first located.

CLAY STREET HILL.—Nearly south of Russian Hill, and about three furlongs from it, rises this hill, the highest within the city limits. It is named from the street which runs just south of its summit, or will do so when cut through. The hill is 376 feet high, and is a little over a mile southwest of Telegraph Hill. The view from its summit differs only in having moved the point of sight a mile southwest, and raised it about 80 feet.

CALIFORNIA STREET HILL—This, too, .takes its name from that of the neighboring street. It is hardly proper to call it a separate hill as it is but two blocks south of Clay Street Hill, from which only a slight hollow originally separated it.

RINCON HILL.—Three quarters of a mile southwest of the City Hall. Its highest point reaches hardly a hundred feet above the bay level. The whole hill originally offered such sightly locations for building that it is covered on nearly all sides, and crowded upon its very height, by some of the most comfortable and home-like residences in the entire city. This fact makes it almost impossible to get an unobstructed view, in all directions, from any part of it. It was a favorite, and almost an aristocratic site for residences, until the heartless greed for gain procured legal authority to excavate the famous " Second Street Cut;" 75 feet deep, which needlessly ruined the beauty of the hill.

LONE MOUNTAIN.—This singularly symmetrical hill stands two and one-half miles west of the City Hall, at the head of Bush street. It is $284\frac{1}{2}$ feet high. From its summit rises a solitary cross which, especially near sunset, stands forth against the western sky with peculiar, beautiful effect. The view hence is full of inspiration and suggestion. None have caught more of these, or embodied them in finer words than Bret Harte, in his favorite lines:

> As I stand by the cross on the lone mountain crest,
>   Looking over the ultimate sea,
> In the gloom of the mountain a ship lies at rest,
>   And one sails away from the lea;
> One spreads its white wings on a far-reaching track,
>   With pennant and sheet flowing free,
> One hides in the shadow with sails laid aback—
>   The ship that is waiting for me!
>
> But lo, in the distance the clouds break away,
>   The Gate's glowing portal I see;
> And I hear, from the out-going ship in the bay,
>   The song of the sailors in glee;
> So I think of the luminous foot-prints that bore
>   The comfort o'er dark Galilee,
> And wait for the signal to go to the shore;
>   To the ship that is waiting for me.

MISSION PEAKS.—The double peaks already mentioned in our panoramic eye-sweep from Telegraph Hill, lying three miles southwest of it, sometimes called the Twin Peaks. They are five hundred and ten feet high, and stand four miles southwest of the City Hall. They are the loftiest points in the county; either summit commands a view which well repays the time and labor expended in gaining it.

BERNAL HEIGHTS.—This name designates a short range of hills nearly five miles west-southwest of the City Hall. Starting near the bay, they run transversely, that is, westerly, for about one mile across the peninsula. Their highest point is two hundred and ninety-five feet above the bay.

The highest point of the Potrero is three hundred and twenty-six feet above low tide, and the San Miguel Hills, near the southerly line of the county, reach the height of about four hundred feet. The Pacific Heights, near Alta Plaza, a mile and a half west of the City Hall, are three hundred and seventy-five feet high.

These are all the natural elevations of note within the city and county. The best artificial outlooks may be had from the roof of the houses standing on or near the summits of those hills which rise within the settled portion. The roof of Bancroft's building, the cupola of the Grand Hotel, the U.S. Military Observatory, on the southwest corner of Third and Market streets, and the Shot Tower, if you can persuade Mayor Selby to let you up, all afford extensive and beautiful prospects.

Having thus told the tourist all we know about the most feasible and temperate methods of " getting high," we leave him to his own direction, only adding that if he isn't satisfied with our efforts in his behalf, he'd better go " up in a balloon," and view our city as the Germans did Paris.

How to get about.

The universal, inexpensive, always-ready and democratic way is by the ever-present Horse Cars. Seven different companies have laid about fifty miles of rail in and about the city, and carry one either directly to or within a very short distance of any desired point.

LINES, ROUTES AND COLORS.—The Omnibus and North Beach and Mission R.R. Companies run yellow cars through Third and Fourth, Sansome, Montgomery and Kearney, the central blocks of Stockton, and the northern ends of Powell and Mason. They also run red cars from the centre of the city to the southwestern limits, through Howard and Folsom streets.

The Central R.R. Co. runs red cars from the steamboat landings along the city front, through Jackson, Sansome, Bush, and other leading streets to Lone Mountain. Their cars are commonly called the Lone Mountain cars.

The Front Street and Ocean R.R. Co. runs green cars from the steamboat landings at the foot of Broadway, up that street, along Battery, Market, Sutter and Polk streets, by Spring Valley to the Presidio, whence 'busses connect for Fort Point. A branch of this road runs through Larkin street across Market through Ninth to Mission; thus connecting the western with the southwestern suburbs. Within the year this company has also constructed and put into operation another branch, carrying one to Laurel Hill Cemetery and Lone Mountain.

The Market Street R.R., the pioneer, runs blue cars from the junction of Montgomery and Market street, opposite the Grand Hotel, through Market by the San José Depot, and out Valencia to Twenty-sixth. From the junction of Ninth and Larkin street with Market, it sends a branch out through Hayes Valley to Hayes Valley Pavilion.

The City R. R.—Lately built, and newly stocked, runs from the west front of Grand Hotel, at the junction of Market and New Montgomery, along the latter to Mission, thence out Mission to Twenty-Sixth, passing directly by the entrance to Woodward's Gardens, and within one block of the San José depot.

The Potrero and Bay View R. R.—Connecting with the North Beach and Mission R. R., at the south end of Fourth street, runs thence across the Long Bridge over Mission Bay—through the Potrero Deep Cut, over the Islais Creek bridge, through South San Francisco to the Bay View Race Track terminus, within half a mile of Hunter's Point and the Dry Dock.

TIMES, FARES, ETC.—Commencing at about 6 P. M., in summer earlier, the cars run at various intervals of from three to seven minutes until 11 and 12 o'clock P. M., and on the City R. R., till 1.30 the next morning. Nearly all the roads sell tickets, having four coupons attached, for twenty-five cents each. Every coupon is good for one fare from one end of the city to the other, and the coupon tickets of one company are received by every other. For single fares, paid without coupons, they usually charge ten cents. Nearly a year ago the City R. R. started the half-dime fare, asking but five cents for a single ride, and the Market street R. R. has also adopted it. "Children occupying seats, full fare."

Several of the companies issue transfer checks entitling the passenger to continue his ride upon any intersecting line without extra charge.

HACKS AND COACHES.—For the benefit of those who have occasion to engage any of the above, for the transient service of any excursion lying outside of the regular routes, or beyond the legal limits within which the fixed fare obtains, we subjoin the following legal regulations also contained in the order and section already quoted on a previous page:

"For a hackney carriage, drawn by more than one horse, for four or less persons, when engaged by the hour, to be computed for the time occupied in going and returning, including detention, $3 for the first hour, and $2 for each subsequent hour.

"For a hackney carriage, drawn by one horse, for two persons, when engaged by the hour, to be occupied in going and returning, including detentions, $1 50 for the first hour, and $1 for each subsequent hour."

It is hardly necessary to remark, yet it may prevent misunderstanding to add, that the above rates pay for the service of the *whole* carriage, and may be equitably divided among the occupants as they agree.

LIVERY SERVICE.—The livery stables of the city are numerous, and well-stocked with animals of blood and speed, and every form of two or four-wheeled vehicles from the substantial, three-seated thorough-braced wagon to the elegant or fancy single buggy or sulky. The usual rates, at all first class stables, are five dollars a day, or a drive, for a single team, and ten dollars for a double one. For a very short trip, and a very short time, they frequently abate something, and when a team is engaged for several days or weeks at once, commonly make the rate lower. For saddle horses the price is usually one half that of a single team, that is $2 50 for a day or drive—subject to similar reductions as above.

ON FOOT.—If you have the nerve and muscle of a man, and are not sadly out of training, by all means walk through or about the city and around its suburbs. In several places, as, in climbing Telegraph or any other hill, you will have to walk, and then you can. Even our lady visitors might profitably emulate the pedestrian performances of their English sisters. Provide good easy, wide-bottomed, low-heeled walking-shoes, boots or gaiters, and take the beautiful, windless and dustless morning hours for it and, unless your taste is fashionably perverted or your physical energy hopelessly exhausted, you will find it most delightful. Among the Scottish Highlands, or in the Swiss Alps, you would certainly do it, endure it, enjoy it, and subsequently boast of it; why not try it here?

Suburbs and Vicinity.

We suppose the visitor to have fairly rested—to have walked about a little through the more central portion; to have somewhat studied the general plan of the city, in view of the larger or shorter time which he has to spend in the city, to have made up his mind how much he will see, and what it shall be. By way of helping his planning and sight-seeing, we now catalogue and briefly remark upon the more notable points, taken in regular order from the most central starting point. We offer the following pages as helpful suggestions to those who cannot avail themselves of the personal guidance of some resident friend, who can constantly accompany them to direct their route, and verbally explain the details which these printed pages attempt. If one has not time, or does not wish to see anything here set down, he can easily omit it, and from the remainder select whatever he may chose, transposing, combining, modifying and adapting according to his own good pleasure.

GENERAL CIRCUIT OF THE CITY.

Commencing at the foot of Market street, thence southward, along or over the water front, continuing around the entire city and returning to the point of starting. Also mentioning more distant points visible to the spectator looking beyond the suburbs:

The Lumber Yards, Wharves and Merchant Fleet, first attract our notice. Millions of feet of boards, plank and timber from the northern coast of this State and from Oregon, ranged in immense piles on broad and deep piers—alongside of which the schooners, brigs and barks of the lumber fleet are constantly discharging.

Thence along Stewart or East street, the latter being nearer the water, by large lumber-yards, boat-shops, blacksmithing and ship-chandling establishments, we reach the California and Oregon S. S. Co's wharves and slips. The Folsom street cars run within five short blocks; nearer than any others.

Black Diamond Coal Company's Pier.—Barges, sheds and piles of coal, straight from the bowels of

Mount Diablo, corner Spear and Harrison streets, P. B. Cornwall, agent.

Rincon Point, foot of Harrison street. The wharves and filling have quite obliterated the old shore line, which originally turning a short corner here, received the name "Rincon," which, in Spanish, means simply a corner.

U. S. Marine Hospital, northwest corner of Harrison and Spear.

P. M. S. S. Co.'s Piers, Docks, Sheds and Slips. Water front, foot of Brannan and Townsend streets. Piers having a total front of 1200 feet, shed 600 feet long by 250 wide. Steamships over five thousand tons register and docks built especially for them. Capt. W. B. Cox, Superintendent.

Gas Works, corner of King and Second. The other works of the same company, the San Francisco Gas Co., are on Howard street, from First to Beale.

C. P. R. R. Co.'s Freight Pier, Depot and Boat. Foot of Second street.

Mission Bay. Foot of Second and Third streets. The broad cove lying between South street and Potrero; now fast filling in, especially beyond, that is, south of the Long Bridge.

Mission Rock.—Off the foot of Third street. Has a shanty on it. Used for fishing.

U. S. Ship Anchorage.—Between foot of Third and the Mission Rock, and within a quarter-mile radius of the latter. U. S. Revenue Cutters and Coast Survey vessels, chiefly occupy it.

Steamboat Reserves.—In the docks between Third and Fourth and the adjacent ones along the south side of the bridge.

Long Bridge.—From the foot of Fourth street, across Mission Bay to Potrero—one mile. Will become Kentucky street, when the filling-in makes a street of what is now a bridge.

Yacht Club Building.—East side of Long Bridge, one third across. Yachts at moorings near.

Potrero.—The point at the south end of Long Bridge. Spanish for pasture ground. Originally a rocky ridge. Fast disappearing under houses.

Glass Works.—Pacific Glass Works, corner Iowa and Mariposa streets, four blocks west of bridge.

Pacific Rolling Mill.—Potrero Point, water front, east of bridge.

Deep Cut, is really Kentucky street, brought down somewhere near the future grade, by cutting through the solid rock, to an average depth of 75 feet for nearly a fifth of a mile.

Rope Walk runs under Kentucky street, near the north end of the Islais Creek Bridge, which is the same street continued across Islais Creek, now a solidly planked bridge, seven eighths of a mile long.

Italian Fishing Fleet and Flakes, on the right of the bridge, along the cove-beach just beyond the rope-walk. Their Mongolian competitors have their boats and beach a little further south.

South San Francisco is the rising land or ridge south of Islais Creek. It is a pleasant suburb, rapidly growing.

Catholic Orphan Asylum, that large, new wooden building fronting on Connecticut street, nine blocks west of the bridge.

Hunter's Point is the east end of South San Francisco, a rocky point in which the Dry Dock, dug out of the solid rock, four hundred and twenty-one feet long, one hundred and twenty feet wide at the top, and sixty feet wide at the bottom, which is twenty-two feet below mean high water. With the Floating Dock, near by, it cost two millions of dollars.

Bay View Race Track, near Railroad Avenue, a mile southwest of Islais Bridge One mile around; broad, smooth and hard. Bay View House at north margin, near west end.

Visitacion Point and Valley, three quarters of a mile beyond the race course; worth driving out to see, if you have plenty of time.

San Bruno Road unites with this railroad avenue about half a mile beyond the race course; brings one back near

New Butchertown, corner of Islais Creek Canal and Kentucky street.

Drive back this old San Bruno Road, until you come to Twenty-sixth street; along that to Mission; down Mission to Seventeenth, out which you may drive until you find your way winding and climbing up and over the east slopes of the peninsular hills along the Ocean House Road, a broad, hard track, leading over the hills to the house which names it. Opposite Twenty-fourth street is the toll gate, where you pay twelve and a half, or twenty-five cents, according to your team. A mile beyond, a side gate, free, admits you to a carriage-way through the fields, leading down, three quarters of a mile, to Lake Honda, the huge double-reservoir of sloping-sided masonry, covered with cement, and holding thirty-five million gallons. This well merits a visit. The City Almshouse stands on the hill, half a mile south of the lake.

The Small-pox Hospital is the small building standing alone on the hill, a third of a mile north of the Almshouse.

Returning to, and resuming the main road, a mile southwesterly and then westerly, brings us to the Ocean Race Course, securely enclosed, and having the usual circuit and surface.

Opposite this, and half a mile south lies Lake Merced, three quarters of a mile long by a fifth of a mile wide. That part of it nearer to, and parallel with the road, is a smaller, nearly separate lake called simply "the Lagoon."

Ocean House, on a slight sandy knoll, half a mile northwest of Lake Merced.

Pacific Beach.—This is the sandy shore of the

"ultimate sea," stretching almost exactly north two miles to the base of the cliff, up which a well-built road carries us a score of rods northwesterly to the

Cliff House, the grand terminus, or at least way-station of all ocean drives. Its broad, covered piazza, well-furnished with easy chairs and good marine glasses, has been for years the popular observatory whence fashion languidly patronizes the Pacific, or gazes with momentary interest upon the

Seal Rocks—three hundred feet from the shore, and dotted with lubberly seals, clumsily climbing upon the lower rocks, or lazily sunning themselves above.

Farallones—Twenty-five miles seaward from the Cliff House—seven sharp-pointed islets break the monotony of the western horizon. The highest of these rises three hundred and forty feet, and has a large lighthouse of the first-class, with the finest Fresnel light on the coast.

Point Lobos, a precipitous coast bluff, a third of a mile north of the Cliff House, chiefly noted as the site of the Signal Station; provided with a fine glass and the usual outfit of a marine observatory. Thence along the beach, or the brow of the bluff, if you like climbing, by the Helmet Rock, whose shape hardly appears from the land, around the curve of the shore, whose general direction here is northeast, a full mile, to

Fort Point, where stands a doubly-strengthened

and heavily-mounted fort, yet unnamed, whose chief interest founds upon its general resemblance to the famous Fort Sumter.

Lighthouse.—The northwest angle of the fort supports a substantial tower, showing a fixed white light. From the walls of the fort, or better still, from the lighthouse balcony, we look upon and across the

Golden Gate, the connecting strait between the Pacific Ocean and San Francisco Bay. It is between three and four miles long, from one to two miles wide, and over four hundred feet deep.

Lime Point, the northern inside gate-post—the southeastern extremity of Marin county.

Point Bonita.—The outer or oceanward point of the northern shore, nearly two miles west of the fort, crowned with a lighthouse.

Mountain Lake—One mile south of the fort, and sending a little rivulet called Lobos Creek westward into the Pacific, which it helps to replenish.

Presidio—Spanish for garrison or barracks. This is nearly a mile southeast of the fort, as we return toward the city. Its main features are the extensive barracks, accommodating several hundred U. S. soldiers, who make this their point of arrival and departure in going to or coming from the different stations to which they may be ordered. Forming the parallelogram front is the parade ground, a broad, open field, gently falling toward the bay, surrounded by the officers' quarters or the barracks, and dotted with batteries here and there.

Black Point.—The water front at the foot of Franklin and Gough streets.

Pioneer Woolen Mills—Corner of Polk and Reade streets. Office, 115 Battery street.

North Beach—From the foot of Powell street west to Black Point.

Angel Island, three and a half miles north of Black Point, across the bay.

Alcatraces Island—A mile and a half north of North Beach, off in the bay, heavily fortified, commanding the Golden Gate.

North Point—Water front, foot of Kearny street, corner of Bay street.

Sea Wall—Water front from the foot of Union street, southward; a sloping bulkhead of rubble, faced with heavier rock, costing $240 a linear foot, and a mile and a half long.

Ferries.—Alameda—Corner of Davis and Pacific street. City Front Cars.

Oakland—Same dock, next slip south. City Front Cars.

Saucelito—Meiggs' Wharf, foot of Powell street. North Beach cars.

San Quentin—Davis street, near Vallejo. City Front or Sutter street cars.

Vallejo—Corner of Front and Vallejo. City Front or Sutter street cars.

HOW TO SEE SAN FRANCISCO AND ITS SURROUNDINGS.

Brief trips, or short excursions, requiring but a few hours each. Short skeleton tours in and about the suburbs, suggesting the most interesting points, with the walks, rides, drives or sails by which one may reach them—the time required and the best hours of the day, the amount of walking necessary, with the conveniences and cost.

IN AND ABOUT THE CITY.

I. Walk up Montgomery street to Telegraph Hill. If you don't feel like climbing clear to the top, follow the foot-path which winds around about two thirds up its east and northeast slopes. If you go to the top you can go down into—or if you take the lower path you will come round into, Lombard street. Walk down that to Powell; turn to your right and follow Powell north to the water and Meiggs' wharf, down the wharf if you want the bay breeze, and the bay sights from a lower level; come back—take the South Park cars; ride up Powell by Washington Square, up Stockton, down Washington—get out at the upper corner of the Plaza, walk diagonally across, notice the old City Hall on your left, stroll up Kearny to California or Bush, down which you descend one block to Montgomery.

II. CHINESE QUARTERS.—Sacramento street, from Kearny to Dupont, along Dupont to Pacific, down

Pacific to Stockton, to Jackson, down Jackson to Kearny; cast your eyes down the little alleyways and courts which cut up the blocks along these streets. Look at these signs! "Hop Yik, Wo Ki, Tin Yuk, Hop Wo, Chung Sun, Cheung Kuong, Hang Ki, Yang Kee, Shang Tong, Shun Wo," that last would'nt be a bad one to go over the door of "civilized" rum-hole. "Wing On Tsiang, Wung Wo Shang, Kwong On Cheang," and scores of others. Most are personal names, some are business mottoes. They are generally phonographic, that is, you pronounce them according to their spelling. Here and there one suggests fun. For instance, "Man Li." Well, why not a Chinaman as well as a white man? Has the superior race the monopoly of lying? That sign is certainly creditable to the Chinese female; it says Man Li; not *woman* lie. Not far thence a very appropriate successor finishes the logical sequence, "Hung Hi." Certainly, why not? That's what ought to be done to any merchant who will lie. Any Man Li, should be "Hung Hi." These celestials certainly have no bad idea of the eternal fitness of things. What would happen to our Melican merchants if that rule were rigidly applied? It would'nt be much trouble to take the next census. This is the out-door glance by daylight. If you want a more thorough exploration by day or by night, call on special officer Duffield, (George

W.) at 1,107 Montgomery street, who knows their haunts and ways, and can show you all you'll care to see. His long experience among them has also acquainted them with him to such a degree, that they allow him to enter and pass through their houses and rooms whence another might be shut out. In fact, he is their special officer, paid by the Chinese merchants to guard their property, and is emphatically *the* man to have for an escort. He can take you into their gambling saloons, into their pigeon-hole lodging houses where rag-pickers, beggars and thieves fill the air with opium smoke, then shove themselves, feet foremost, into a square box of a pigeon-hole, more like a coffin than a couch. He can guide you into crooked, narrow, labyrinthine passages through which you can just squeeze, and which you could never find nor enter without guidance; into inner courts, around which, and in the midst of which, stand old rickety, tumble-down, vermin-haunted hives of wooden tenements which rise through three or four stories, all alive with the swarming lazzaroni, packed into the smallest and dirtiest of rooms, and huddled into every dark and filthy corner.

These are the lowest and worst of their race; the *infernal* celestials, among whom the officer will not take a woman at all, and where it would not be safe for any man to attempt entrance alone. The approaches are so ingeniously constructed and so art-

fully disguised, and the passages wind among each
other so intricately, and intersect each other so per-
plexingly, that not one in a thousand could ever
find the beginning, and hardly one in ten thousand
could discover the end.

> "For *ways* that are *dark*,
> And for *tricks* that are *vain*,
> The heathen Chinee *is* peculiar;
> Which the same I would rise to explain."

The stranger must not conclude, however, that
such as these make up the bulk of the Chinese who
come to us. On the contrary, these are the lowest
and vilest, the dregs and settlings of their social
system; no more fit to be taken as samples of their
nation than the low, whisky-drinking, shillaly-
swinging, skull-cracking, vote-repeating Irish, who
now govern New York, are to be taken as fair types
of the "finest pisantry undher the sun," or considered as a representative of the educated Irishman,
than whom a warmer-hearted, freer-handed, more
courteous-mannered gentleman one can hardly meet
in a thousand miles.

So the middle classes of the Chinese are cleanly,
sober, industrious and honest, while their leading
merchants, of whom we have several fine represen-
tatives in the city, are models of business integrity
and social courtesy. Enter one of their establishments, with proper introduction, and you shall encounter the most perfect politeness throughout the

interview, and carry away the impression that you were never more heartily welcomed and generously entertained, according to their custom, of course, by *any* strangers, in your life.

And one very notable thing should also be said of their street deportment; you may walk through their quarter every day and night for a month, and not see a single drunken man of their own race. If you encounter one at all, he is likely to belong to the "superior race."

Your survey of the Chinese quarter would be incomplete without a visit to their temples or joss houses. One of these stands off Pine, just above Kearny. They are also used as hospitals.

Should you wish any souvenir in the shape of their peculiarly ingenious manufacture, you may find them at the Chinese or Japanese bazaars.

III. THIRD STREET.—Five and a half blocks to South Park; thence three blocks to the water; along Channel street to Long Bridge. Here we may take the Bay View cars, ride across the Mission Bay, visit the Rolling Mills, or keep on through the Deep Cut, over Islais Creek bridge, through South San Francisco, to Bay View track, whence 'busses carry us to Hunter's Point and the Dry Dock. Best time, morning, unless some ship is going into dock on the high tide. Fare in 'bus, twenty-five cents each.

IV.—WATER FRONT–South of Market.–Walk along East or Stewart St., by U. S. Marine Hospital, to P. M.S.S. Co.'s ships and docks and C. P.R.R. Freight piers and depot. Thus far no cars. At foot of Brannan take cars, ride up that to Third, down Third, by South Park, to Howard—along Howard to Second, along Second to Market again. Or you can walk from the water up Second to Market again. Or you can walk from the water up Second through the cut to Harrison, climb the bridge-stairs, walk down Harrison to First or Fremont, turn left, and come back by the Shot Tower, Foundries, and Factories to Market.

V.—WATER FRONT—North of Market.—No cars here. Stroll northerly by the corners of the different streets, along the heads of the different piers, among the grain and produce boats, river steamer docks and ferry slips, around to North Point, with its bonded warehouses, iron clippers, and sea wall, thence back Sansome to Broadway, whence cars take you again to the centre.

VI.—SOUTHWESTERN SUBURBS.—From corner west front of Grand Hotel, take city cars out Mission, by fine new church, new Mint, to Woodward's Gardens; thence to Sixteenth; up that three blocks, westerly, to Dolores street, where stands the old Mission Church, the site of the first permanent settlement of San Francisco; out Dolores; south two blocks, to Jewish Cemeteries; back by same way to

Sixteenth; down that to Mission Woolen Mills; thence home by Folsom street or Howard street cars, either of which brings you to Market street.

VII.—WESTERN SUBURBS and beyond.—From Montgomery up Sutter, by cars, or up Bush by feet or wheels. Either street carries you westerly to Laurel Hill, in which elegant monuments and mausoleums merit more than passing notice; thence east three blocks to Lone Mountain and the cemeteries grouped about its base, and upon its lower slopes—the Odd Fellows', west; the Masonic, south, and the Calvary north and east. Out the Cliff House Road—you'll need horse probably, or can take the 'bus for 25 cents each way—by the Race Track or Driving Park, to the Cliff House; look at the Seal Rocks, Seals, Ocean and Farallones; thence south along Pacific Beach to Ocean House, whence in by Ocean Road or the new Central Road by Lake Peralta and Lake Honda. The old Ocean Road brings you back through the Mission; the new one, in by Lone Mountain again.

VIII.—NORTHWESTERN SUBURBS and beyond.—Up Geary, Post or Sutter to Van Ness Avenue; thence twelve blocks north through Spring Valley, by cars from Broadway west to Harbor View, Presidio and Fort Point. Returning from the Presidio, keep towards the Bay; come around by Black Point, whence, skirting the water-front through five or six rough blocks, you reach the foot of Mason or Powell street, and find other cars waiting to bring you home.

The routes above suggested, are by no means exhaustive, but will take one to or near the most noted points. If the tourist can have the personal guidance and escort of some well-posted friend, so much the better. In the absence of such friend, or even to accompany him, we respectfully submit our little pocket substitute.

EXCURSION ROUTES.

Under this head we suggest different excursions to and through the most noted localities within a limited radius. We have arranged them in the order of their neighborhood to each other, so that one may pass from the end of one to the beginning of the next without the necessity of returning to San Francisco more than once or twice before completing them all.

I. The Bay Trip.

We suppose you tired of land travel, with its accompanying jar and dust, and willing to spend a half day in a smooth-sailing steamer on the beautiful bay. Go to No. 703 Market street, only nine nine doors east of Bancroft's, to the office of Gen. Ord, commanding the Department of California. He can give you a pass, ordering the captain of the McPherson, the lively little Government propeller, which daily makes the rounds of the military posts on all the chief islands in the harbor, to take you to any you may wish to visit, or all, if you desire. No other boat makes these trips. This one goes the rounds twice a day. Unless particularly fond of high wind, and short, choppy, sea-sicky waves, you'd better go in the morning. The steamer leaves Jackson street pier every morning at eight, and every afternoon at three. It takes you first, to

ALCATRAZ, or Alcatraces, as the Government spells it over the fortress gate. The first is the singular, and the second the plural, form of a Spanish word meaning a pelican. The island lies a mile and a quarter north of San Francisco, and two and one half miles east of the Golden Gate, whose entrance it commands. It is one third of a mile long, one tenth of a mile wide, rises a hundred and forty feet above low tide; a rudely elongated oval in shape, contains about thirty acres, composed mainly of solid rock; is heavily fortified on all sides and crowned by a strong fortress on the top. Perfect belts of batteries surround the island, mounting some of the heaviest guns yet made in America. It is the key to the fortifications of the harbor.

The island affords no fresh water. All which is used there is carried thither from the main land or caught in cisterns during the rainy season. On the highest point stands a lighthouse of the third order, whose light can be seen, on a clear night, twelve miles at sea, outside the Golden Gate.

The southeast point of the island has a heavy fog-bell, which strikes four times a minute through all dense fogs. If you wish to land and examine the fortress and batteries, you can do so, and stay until the boat returns, usually half or three quarters of an hour, or remain till its afternoon trip, five or six hours later. From Alcatraz, the boat goes a mile and a half to

ANGEL ISLAND, which lies three miles north of San Francisco, and is the largest and most valuable island in the bay. It is a mile and one third long, three quarters of a mile wide, and seven hundred and seventy-one feet high. It contains about six hundred acres of excellent land, watered by natural springs. On the east side are quarries of blue and brown sand-stone, while good brick-clay is found elsewhere. Three fixed batteries, mounting large and heavy guns, and connected by a military road encircling the island, have been built. The officers' quarters, barracks, and parade ground, are in a shallow, gently-sloping valley, near the landing on the west side.

Returning, we touch at Alcatraz and thence steam round to

YERBA BUENA, or Goat Island, two miles east of San Francisco, and two and a half from the Oakland shore, from which the long railroad pier is heading straight for it, with the evident intention of bridging the entire distance at an early day.

The island contains little over half a square mile, principally covered with chapparal, which is here a thicket of low, evergreen oaks, dwarfed by the salt air and the high winds. The Government also owns and occupies this island—barracks, shops, and garrison. The name Goat Island was given from the fact that many vessels coming to this port in early times, from southern ports where goats were cheap, used to bring them for fresh meat on the passage. In the event of a short voyage, a few goats survived, and upon arrival here were turned loose upon this island, as it lay near the anchorage, and provided a place from which the goats could not escape. These veteran survivors of the voyage "round the horn," presently increased to such numbers as to originate the name "Goat Island," which has, to a considerable degree, supplanted the earlier and more significant name Yerba Buena. This latter name, having been lifted from the city, ought at least to be allowed to fall and rest upon the island, in perpetuation of those "early days," whose landmarks are fast failing and fading into forgetfulness.

Now return with the boat to the pier, exchange the pure bay-breeze for dust-laden city airs, and you have completed your bay trip.

II. The Oakland Trip.

OAKLAND lies seven miles east of San Francisco. At least that is the distance from centre to centre; between the nearest margins the measure would be hardly five miles. A dozen times a day the ferryboat takes one over; fare, 25 cents. Get out at Broadway street, turn to your left, walk four or five blocks, notice the comfortable, roomy appearance of the city. Two blocks up, observe that neat church on the left, set well back from the street and surrounded by ample grounds and pleasant gardens. That's Rev. Dr. Mooar's Congregational Church. A block or two beyond, look up the broad street to the right, and you see the buildings and grounds now occupied by the State University of California, pending the erection of ampler accommodations on the University site at Berkeley, five miles north. Take the horse cars if you like, and ride out north along the "telegraph road." Noble residences and beautiful grounds line both sides of the way. A mile out, that large, new, wooden building, crowning the summit of a moderate hill, accommodates McClure's Academy, wherein the military drill reinforces and enlivens the other usual studies of a first-class academy.

A third of a mile further, upon the same side appears the large and finely-proportioned Pacific Female College, lately purchased by the Pacific Theological Seminary.

Still north two miles further, brings us to or in front of the

Deaf, Dumb and Blind Asylum, beautifully located on the top of a little rise, and commanding a fine view of the Golden Gate, the bay, San Francisco, and its surroundings. The style of the building is a modified Gothic. It is built of a fine-grained, bluish granite, from a neighboring quarry. It has a length of one hundred and ninety-two feet front, one hundred and forty-eight feet depth, sixty-two feet height up the three stories and a half to the gable, and one hundred and forty-five feet to the top of the tower. Within, the school-rooms, chapel, halls, dormitories, and bath-rooms, are models of convenient arrangement. Principal, Prof. Wilkinson.

Another mile and we cross a ravine, bear away to the left, and find ourselves on the grounds of the State University of which only the Mining and Agricultural College Building has begun to take form. The site is the finest imaginable: facing the Golden Gate, the bay and its islands, and the "Golden City" beyond.

Continuing west from the University site, we may go down to the San Pablo road and return to Oakland by a different route. Approaching the centre we may note the new City Hall, delight ourselves with glances down the broad and "tree-ful" streets. Arrived at the Market street station we take the cars south, cross the San Antonio creek, through Brooklyn to San Leandro, where we may get out and take another train to

Hayward's,

Six miles southeasterly from San Leandro. This is a new, pleasantly-situated and rapidly-growing town, the shipping point for a large agricultural region around. Here see the grain sheds, run out to the Brighton cattle market, the largest in the State, after which you can take stage·six miles to

Alvarado,

And there inspect the salt works, but, more especially, the

Beet Sugar Works, the first erected and operated in California, and regarded as the pioneer of an extensive and valuable industry. From Alvarado you can keep on, by stage, nine miles to the

WARM SPRINGS, or you can reach these by driving to Niles, or Decoto, and thence taking the cars of the San José road. These springs are about two miles south of the Old Mission San José, in the midst of a pleasant grove of oak and other trees, near the Agua Caliente (hot water) creek. The waters contain lime, sulphur, magnesia, and iron, in various combinations. Summer guests speak highly of the neighboring hotel.

From the springs return to the railroad, and riding eleven miles, enter on

IV. The San Jose Trip.

which begins with

San Jose.

The county seat of Santa Clara county; in population the fourth city of the State, in character of population one of the first, and in beautiful surroundings the gem city. It has a fine situation, in the midst of a beautiful valley, and a climate so healthy that many people affected with lung complaints go thither to live, as a means of cure. Hundreds from San Francisco and the intermediate cities, go on excursions to San José and vicinity every summer. From whatever direction we approach San José, the first object to meet the eye is the lofty dome of the

Court House. Next to the State Capitol at Sacramento, this is the finest building in the State. It stands on the west side of First street, fronting St. James Square. Its architecture is Roman Corinthian; its dimensions, one hundred feet front, one hundred and forty feet depth; height, fifty-six feet to cornice; to top of dome, one hundred and fifteen feet. The building is divided into two lofty stories, containing the principal court room, sixty-five feet long, forty-eight feet wide and thirty-eight feet high, with twenty large and elegant rooms for county officials. The view from the dome is alone worth going to San José to enjoy. Whatever else you may omit, in and about the city, do *not* omit this.

THE STATE NORMAL SCHOOL BUILDING. Next to the Court House, this is the chief object of interest. It occupies the centre of Washington Square, faces west; architecture, Corinthian; length, two hundred and eighty-four feet; depth, one hundred and sixty feet; and height to top of cornice, seventy feet; to top of tower, one hundred and fifty-two feet; number of stories, four, including basement and mansard roof. The Normal Hall is ninety-one feet long, sixty-six feet wide, and forty feet high, accommodating nine hundred.

AUZERAIS HOUSE. Among the finest buildings in the city, and the best hotel south of San Francisco, is the Auzerais House. For first-class hotel accommodations in all variety, for cordial welcome and courteous service, stop here, and you will not be disappointed; especially when restfully reclining in the charming park and garden attached to the house. Rates, usual first-class; from $3.00 single day, to $20.00, or even $15.00, a week, with lower rates for longer times.

NEW YORK EXCHANGE HOTEL. Corner of First and St. John's streets, ranking next to the Auzerais, affords excellent rooms, with good board and attentive service, for from $2.00 a day to $12.00 a week.

If you want to ride through the surrounding valley, as you certainly will, after looking from the court-house dome, go to Church & Wallace, No. 386 First street, who will have a capital team waiting for you at the station if you merely drop them a slight hint by telegraph.

Besides the public buildings already named, fine churches, school buildings, business blocks, private residences and beautiful gardens well repay a stroll through this queen city of a lovely valley.

New Almaden.

From San José, take one of Church & Wallace's teams, and drive thirteen miles southerly to the celebrated

Quicksilver Mine, named for the famous old Almaden mine, in Spain, with the syllable, " new," prefixed by way of distinction. This mine is over five hundred feet deep, and employs nearly five hundred men. For permission to enter, apply to J. B. Randol, Esq., manager, residing at New Almaden. If you prefer to go out by public conveyance, a stage will take you over any afternoon at 2.30 for $1.50.

Drive back to San José: thence, by steam car, horse car or private team, go over three miles north to

Santa Clara,

A pleasant, quiet town, chiefly noted for the Santa Clara College (Jesuit), which occupies the site of the old mission, which was really the germ of the town; and the University of the Pacific (Methodist).

Saratoga.

Springs, of course, ten miles southwest of San José, from which daily stage carries one over for $1.50. These springs are called the

Congress Springs, from the resemblance of their water to that of the original and famous springs of that name at the New York Saratoga. They are three shallow springs, excavated in the sandstone, and tasting very much alike. The water contains sulphates and carbonates of soda, iron and lime, with traces of magnesia. It is very refreshing and healthful; so much so that the guests at the neighboring hotel annually consume increasing quantities, besides the thousand bottles sent away daily.

Thence back to San José, and, after a good night's rest, set forth on tour·

V. Gilroy, and Points South,

and the places for which it is the starting point.

This brisk and lively, neat and thriving town, we beg its pardon, *city*, is thirty-one miles southeast of San José, from which one reaches it by the

Southern Pacific Railroad for a fare of $2.00. This city is the present terminus of the railroad, and the consequent centre from which radiate the various stage routes to the " lower country." On every hand it presents evidences of business prosperity and rapid growth. Population, over two thousand.

Hot Spring—Fourteen miles northeast of Gilroy, in a small, rocky ravine opening into Coyote Cañon, is this noted spring. Its water contains iron, soda, magnesia, sulphur, and baryta, and has a pungent but not unpleasant taste. Throughout the year it preserves a uniform temperature of about one hundred and ten degrees. Within a rod of the hot spring are a dozen or more large springs of pure, cold water. The curative properties of the water, added to the romantic character of the surrounding scenery, have caused the erection of a fine hotel, reached by regular stages, over a good road, from Gilroy.

Some twelve miles southwest of Gilroy, one may find, in the

Pajaro Valley,

As quiet and beautiful an agricultural nook as the State affords. For a quiet retreat in some hospitable farmhouse, with a good chance for small game, for a day or two, this snug valley will decidedly "fill the bill." Its black soil, famous potatoes, and charming little branch cañons will dispose a farmer, or a hunter, or a painter to stay as long as possible. When you have rusticated as long as you can in the romantic vicinity of Gilroy, and are ready, though unwilling, to go, you can return by the way you came, if you like; but, if time permits, and you wish to see one of the pleasantest sections of the State, you will take stage through Hollister and

San Juan,

A quiet little town, old and quaint, and chiefly notable for its early mission, founded in 1797, to

Monterey,

The first capital of California, and noted, also, as the place where the American flag was first raised in California, by Com. Sloat, July 7th, 1846. Here one may see plenty of the old adobe houses, with tiled roofs, built in the primitive Mexican style. From Monterey, you may come up the coast, by water, or go back to San Juan, and thence take stage to Watsonville, near the seaward end of the beautiful Pajaro Valley, and come through to

VI. Santa Cruz, and Up the Coast.

Beyond comparison the most delightful among the smaller towns of the State. In fact it is the occidental Newport, the Pacific Nahant, where languid fashion and exhausted business most do congregate. Here land and water meet, present the best beauty of each, and combine to proffer new ones impossible to either alone. Rides, rambles and drives, swims and sails, picnics and chowder-parties, excellent hotel accommodations, and plenty of good company, furnish the material for as varied enjoyment, and as much of it, as any one of ordinary constitution can stand. The way of approach which we have mentioned, is comparatively rare. The most noted route is from Santa Clara by daily stage, thirty miles; fare, $3.20.

When you have sufficiently enjoyed Santa Cruz and its beautiful surroundings, you may take the stage any Monday, Wednesday or Friday morning, at eight o'clock, for a

Ride Up the Coast

Eight miles north we pass Laguna Creek, noted for good fishing, while its vicinity proffers fine shooting, both of which attractions have combined to make it a favorite camping-ground for picnic parties.

Nearly three miles further, William's Landing gives you the first chance to witness "hawser-shipping", an ingenious device for getting produce, or any form of merchandise, into a boat, or upon the deck of a vessel when the surf is too rough to permit the landing of a boat or the continuance of a pier. Thus art makes a "port" for loading or discharging where nature forbids the construction of the ordinary facilities.

Three and a half miles brings us to Davenport's Landing, an open roadstead, famous for the longest pier running out into the open ocean, of any place on the Pacific Coast.

Thence two miles, to the beautiful laurel groves and camping grounds of Scott's Creek. Nearly one hundred and fifty deer have been killed in this neighborhood in one season.

Four miles more, and Frogtown welcomes us. Here David Post proves himself posted in the providing of "good square" meals; in fact, he's just the David who can slay the Goliah of hunger, though, instead of hitting one in the middle of the forehead, he commonly aims about an inch below the nose.

Waddell's Wharf is three miles further. Thence, by Steel's Ranch and White House Ranch to

Pigeon Point.

On the coast, about ten miles from Frogtown, thirty-one from Santa Cruz, and seven from Pescadero. This is important to all the neighboring inhabitants, because it is their shipping point, where one may witness the "hawser-pier" in its glory; and interesting to the tourist, because it is a whaling station, and the only one on the coast which he will be likely to see. A colony of Portuguese do the whaling. They go out in large open boats, six men to a boat, and shoot the harpoon into the whale from the harpoon-gun. One may sometimes see a dozen or more whales at once, rolling and spouting, or "blowing," in the offing.

Seven miles further, and our journey ends, or, at least, this particular stage-route ends in

Pescadero.

Ho for Pescadero and the famous Pebble Beach! By rail from San Francisco to San Mateo, twenty miles south, thence by Troy coaches over a new toll road, to Pescadero, thirty miles. Total distance, fifty miles. Time: to San Mateo, one hour, thence to Pescadero, four and a half hours. Fare: to San Mateo, $1.00, thence to Pescadero, $2.85.

Leaving San Mateo, the road winds through beautiful scenery to the summit of the Santa Cruz mountains, which divide the waters of the Bay from those of the ocean. The summit is eight miles from San Mateo and affords a view of great extent, embracing the long coast line on the west, white with the surf of breakers, and the broad expanse of the Bay on the east, with the Diablo range of mountains bounding the horizon.

From the summit, it is four miles to the old-fashioned pueblo of Spanishtown, nestled in a little dell opening out on Half-Moon Bay. Thence four miles to Purissima, another coast town, near which an isolated, rounded peak, called Ball Knob, rises conspicuously above the surrounding hills. From

Purissima, a drive of twelve miles along, or in sight of, the beach, brings us to our destination.

Pescadero, is the Spanish for fisherman, from *pescado*, fish. The town is situated near the mouth of Pescadero creek, so named, probably, from the abundance of trout which swarm in its pools and eddys. The village is about a mile from the beach, in a sheltered depression, affording a charming and secluded retreat for pleasure seekers and invalids. The tourist will find good hotel and stabling accommodations, among the best of which are the Lincoln hotel and stables, under the charge of Capt. Kinsey.

Prominent among the objects of interest around Pescadero, is the celebrated Pebble Beach, three miles south. Here may be seen ladies, gentlemen, and children, on a warm summer day, down on their hands and knees, searching for curious and pretty little pebbles of every hue and shape. The supply is never exhausted, for every storm casts up a new store of treasures. Pebbles of sufficient beauty and value to be set in brooches and rings, have been discovered here.

The Shell Beach is two miles further on, being five miles from the hotel, and affords a great deal of variety to the beach hunters.

The Moss Beach is twelve miles south, and here the lovers of the most beautiful, fanciful and delicate combinations of colors and fibres, peculiar to sea mosses, can revel to their hearts' content.

The other objects of interest along the coast, are Sea Lion Rocks, two miles west of the hotel, being, as the name suggests, a large rock covered with sea lions.

Marble Bath Tubs, five miles south. These are excavations in the solid rock, in the shape of bath tubs, some of natural and some of colossal size.

Pescadero Creek, as above intimated, is a noted trouting stream. A beautiful drive of six miles up the creek, brings us to the Mineral Springs, and two miles further, is a forest of Big Trees, some of which are said to be fifty feet in circumference. In their vicinity are three shingle mills.

One mile west of the town, is a so-called Indian Mound, from the summit of which a fine view is obtained.

The Butano Falls seven miles distant, on Butano Creek, consists of a succession of cascades, over thirty feet high, located in a deep ravine, surrounded by romantic scenery.

From Pescadero, we may keep on up the coast, any Monday, Wednesday or Friday morning, through San Gregorio, Purissima, and other quiet little towns, through a beautiful country, over high hills and bluffs bordering on the beach, and affording most magnificent ocean views, eighteen miles, to Spanishtown, or

Half Moon Bay.

The shipping-point of a fertile region lying in the immediate vicinity, and extending back into branching valleys.

From this place the road leaves the coast, climbs the hills, by a winding and well-cut grade, to a height of eight hundred feet, whence one enjoys a combination of bay, ocean, hill and valley scenery rarely equaled. Upon this summit we pass, for convenience' sake, to

Crystal Springs and San Mateo County,

and, after enjoying four miles of charming views, while winding down the western slopes, we reach

Crystal Springs, where a number of cold, clear springs break through the rocks, in a romantic cañon, forming so attractive a spot for summer recreation that a large and fine hotel has been built and well sustained. The neighboring roads are good, the tramps endless, and game encouragingly plentiful. Thence four miles of delightful road brings us to

San Mateo,

And the iron track again. This is a beautiful little town, made expressly for homes. Several prominent San Francisco merchants have here hidden their country residences away among oak groves so snugly that one must know exactly where they are, and even then be close upon them, before he would begin to suspect their number, their beauty, and their comfort.

From this place, it is worth one's while to drive or ride four miles down to

Belmont,

Noted as a favorite picnic ground for large Sunday school and society excursions, chiefly from San Francisco, and as the residence of Wm. C. Ralston, Esq., whose country seat, in beauty of location, extent of accommodations, with variety and completeness of appointments, happily combines the elegance of a palace with the simplicity and comfort of a home. Many a distinguished eastern visitor warmly remembers the generous hospitality of that "home behind the hill."

From Belmont, it is but three miles and a quarter to

Redwood City,

The county seat of San Mateo county, on a navigable slough leading into the bay. Its chief industry is the hauling from the hills and shipping from the wharves the redwood lumber, whose abundance has named the town. It has a good hotel—the American House. Four miles south of Redwood City,

Menlo Park

Terminates our excursion in this direction. The attractions of this place are the fine residences of San Francisco merchants, surrounded by noble oaks, which, scattered and grouped over a square mile or two, hereabout, have furnished half the name of the place. Nature made it a "Park;" man added the "Menlo."

Here we may take the cars again, and after a ride of thirty-two miles, first passing, in reverse order, through the three towns just named, with Millbrae, the elegant home of D. O. Mills, Esq., San Bruno, Twelve Mile Farm, Schoolhouse Station and San Miguel, we complete the southern tour around the bay and along the coast, and again commit ourselves for a time to the whirl and dust and bustle of the metropolis.

Having refreshed ourselves with a dash of city life again for a day or two, we are off for the northern circuit, including San Rafael, Mt. Tamalpais, San Quentin, State Prison, and Saucelito. No. 9: Petaluma, Santa Rosa, Healdsburg, the Geysers, and Clear Lake, with Sonoma and its vineyards, we complete No. 10 with Vallejo, Mare Island, the U. S. Navy Yard, Napa, Napa Valley, Oak Knoll and Calistoga. We come back down the valley to Vallejo, whence McCue's stages take us to Benicia, seven and a half miles.

• [For particulars of above three trips, see Bancroft's Tourist's Guide—Geysers.]

11. Mt. Diablo Trip.

Across the strait of Carquinez from Benicia, and connected with it by a steam ferry, lies

Martinez,

The county seat of Contra Costa county. The town has a picturesque situation, several pleasant residences, very beautiful surroundings, and a charming climate. The celebrated Alhambra ranch, which has taken several medals as the best cultivated farm, yielding the best fruits, and the best native wine in the State, lies but a short distance hence. Five miles back from Martinez and the bay, connected with the former by stage and with the latter by a navigable creek, stands

Pacheco,

A quiet, pleasant, country town, noted as the shipping point of the broad and fertile agricultural fields of the Diablo and San Ramon valleys, lying around and beyond it. The manufacture of carriages and agricultural implements also conduce to its prosperity and importance. Another daily stage line also connects this town with Oakland.

Eight miles beyond Pacheco, further in and higher up, is

Clayton,

The largest and most romantically situated town in this part of the State, and in the latter particular, surpassed by few on the coast. Occupying an elevated bench, or plateau, it commands fine views, and having many wide-spreading oaks scattered through and around, it posesses much intrinsic beauty. Mr. Clayton, whose name the town has taken, has a vineyard of nearly forty thousand vines, which, though never irrigated, are vigorous and prolific. He sends his excellent grapes directly to San Francisco, for the immediate market which they are sure to command, and thus realizes a greater profit than by making them into wine. Other vineyards and orchards in this vicinity have over one hundred thousand vines, and nearly forty thousand fruit trees. Clayton is the usual point of departure for the ascent of

Mount Diablo,

Three thousand eight hundred and seventy-six feet high, and christened with its infernal appellation because, like its satanic prototype, it seldom lets men out of its sight. The best time to climb the mountain is early in the morning—the earlier the better. If one can stand on the summit at sunrise he will receive the most ample reward for his early rising. The distance from Clayton up is eight miles; the time occupied by a comfortable ascent is a little over two hours. If there are ladies, or persons unused to riding and climbing, the party should allow a good three hours. The Clayton livery stable furnishes trained saddle horses for $2.50 a day. The expense of a guide, who furnishes his own horse, is $4.00 for the trip, which, of course, as in Yosemite, is usually divided among the party. Though not absolutely necessary to employ a guide, it is decidedly safer and better, especially if the party includes ladies, as the trail is in some places difficult, and even dangerous. to strangers. The first four miles south from Clayton a good carriage-road follows the course of a stream through a deep cañon. Over this part, ladies unused to the saddle, and desiring to avoid unnecessary fatigue, would better ride on wheels. At the end of this road, near a farm-house, the tourist turns to the right, and follows a cut trail westerly to Deer Flat, where are two huts and a spring. Beyond Deer Flat, the trail runs south-easterly to the top of a ridge in sight of the flat below, and thence lies along the top of this ridge, two and a half miles to the summit, where, for the first time in his life, probably, the traveler may get the devil fairly under his feet—or at least the devil's mountain.

In the opinion of most tourists, this peak commands a more extensive, varied, and beautiful prospect than any equal elevation in the world. The mountain has two peaks, lying in a northeast and southwest line, nearly three miles apart. The southwestern one is the higher, and possesses scientific or topographical interest, from the fact that the State Survey made it one of the three "initial points," from which they ran the "base lines" and "meridian lines," from which or by which the townships and sections are reckoned and located in all extensive conveyances of land. This mountain has an additional claim to its sulphurous surname, from the fact that it is supposed to have been, formerly, a volcano.

Looking east upon a clear day, or with the good field glass which some one of the party has thoughtfully provided, you may see the Pacific Ocean, sometimes the Farallone Islands, San Francisco, the bay, the Golden Gate, Mt. Tamalpais, the Petaluma, Sonoma and Napa Valleys, San Pablo and Suisun Bays, Vallejo, Navy Yard, Benicia, the Sacramento and San Joaquin Valleys, with the tortuous windings of their serpentine rivers, creeks and sloughs, Stockton and Sacramento cities, the Marysville Buttes, and the snow-capped Sierras beyond all; while away to the southwest the quiet Santa Clara valley completes the magnificent sweep of the glorious panorama, unrolled for more than a hundred miles around.

If any of the party feel like sermonizing, the text

will readily occur to you: "Then the Devil taketh him up into an exceeding high mountain, and showeth him all the kingdoms of the world, and the glory of them, and saith unto him: ' All these things will I give thee if thou wilt fall down and worship me." As for his proposition to "fall down," we have only to remark, "Beloved hearers! don't you do it, for the devil or any other man;" you'd break your necks as sure as you tried it. Better *sit* down in one of the sheltered nooks in the lee below the summit, eat your lunch and prepare for the descent.

We may easily return to Clayton in time to visit the

Black Diamond Coal Mines,

At Nortonville, six miles distant, over a good road, through a rugged, mountainous and picturesque region. The tunnels enter the northeast side of the mountain, descend nearly three hundred feet southwesterly, whence one level follows a three-foot-thick seam, a good half mile northwesterly. Two main seams are worked at present, one four feet and the other about three feet thick. They dip easterly, or northeasterly. The mine is very neat, and even cleanly, for a coal mine, so that one *could* wear down an ordinary suit without harmful soiling.

The railroad from the mine to the pier, five miles and a half below, whither iron cars, propelled by gravity, can carry three thousand tons per day, is chiefly remarkable for its unusual grade down the first mile and a half, through which the descent is two hundred and seventy-four feet to the mile. To meet this unusual, but unavoidable necessity, heavy locomotives, of peculiar design and construction, were invented and built at San Francisco. They weigh twenty tons, have three pairs of thirty-six-inch driving wheels, with complex and powerful brakes for the enormous friction necessary.

From these mines one may descend by the railroad already described, to New York Landing, whence the regular Stockton steamer will transport him thither, or return him to San Francisco, the tourist's grand base of supplies, and point of departure for nearly all the more notable excursions about the State and the coast.

12. Sacramento, Stockton, and the Lakes.

To the eleven tours already detailed, one may, or even must, add a twelfth, which is separated from the others, and added, in conclusion, because it consists of cities and places lying on or near the great overland route by which every tourist will be almost certain to enter or leave the State; in most cases, both. These are the capital city, Sacramento; the San Joaquin county seat, Stockton; with Lake Tahoe and Donner lake. One may stop to see these as he comes or goes, or may make them the objects of a special excursion, of which the two lakes, especially Tahoe, are notably worthy.

Sacramento.

At the time of the American occupation of California, and for some time previous, the present site of this city was called the "Embarcadero;" that is, in Spanish, simply "the wharf, or the landing-place," though it strictly means the shipping-place.

Gen. Jno. A. Sutter came from New Mexico and settled here in August, 1839. The next year the Mexican Government granted him the land on which he had "located." He accordingly built a fort and gave himself to stock raising, agriculture, and trade. Thenceforward for several years the place was known only as "Sutter's Fort." In July, 1845, Gen. Sutter engaged the service of Jas. W. Marshall, as a sort of agent, or manager. This man became the discoverer of gold in the following accidental manner: In September, 1847, he went up some fifty miles from the fort, upon the south fork of the American river, to construct a sawmill, which, in due time, with one single, most fortunate blunder, he accomplished. The blunder was this: when the water was let on, the tail-race proved too narrow and too shallow. To widen and deepen it in the quickest and cheapest way, he let through a strong current of water, which swept a mass of mud and gravel down to and beyond the lower end.

January 19th, 1848, the birth-day of the "Golden Age" in California, Marshall noticed several yellowish particles shining out from this mud and gravel. He was, naturally, curious enough to collect and examine them. He called five carpenters who were at work on the mill, to join their judgments with his. They talked over the *possibility* of its being gold, but seem to have thought it so little *probable*, that they quietly returned to their usual work. Among the larger pieces of "yellow stuff" which Marshall picked up that day, was a pebble weighing six pennyweights and eleven grains. He gave it to the nearest housekeeper, Mrs. Weimer, and asked her to boil it in saleratus water and see what would come of it. She was making soap at the time, and thinking the lye would prove stronger than simple saleratus water, she immediately pitched it into the soap kettle, from which it was fished out the next day, and found all the brighter for its long boiling.

Two weeks later, Marshall brought the specimens down to the fort and gave them to Sutter to have them tested. Before the General had quite made up his mind as to whether they were certainly gold or not, he went up to the mill, and, with Marshall, made a treaty with the Indians, buying their titles to all the surrounding country. The little circle that knew it, tried to keep the matter secret, but it soon leaked out, and though not sure of its real nature, several began to hunt the yellow stuff that might prove the king of metals.

The next month, February, one of the party carried some of the dust down to Yerba Buena (San Francisco). Here he providentially met Isaac Humphrey, an old Georgia gold miner, who, upon his first look at the specimens, said they were gold, and that the diggings must be rich. He tried to persuade some of his friends to go up to the mill with him, but they thought it only a crazy expedition, and let him go alone. Mr. Humphrey reached the mill March 7th. Only a few were lazily hunting for gold; there was no excitement; the most of the men were working in the mill as usual. Next day he began "prospecting," and quickly satisfied himself that he had "struck it rich." He returned to the mill, made a "rocker," and immediately commenced placer mining in dead earnest.

A few days later, Baptiste, a Frenchman, who had mined in Mexico, left the lumber he was sawing for Sutter, at Weber's, ten miles east of Coloma, and came over to the mill. He agreed with Humphrey that the region was rich, furnished himself with rocker and pan, and forthwith began to develop the shining wealth, beside which mills, lumber, ranches, flocks, and crops were of small account. So these two men, Humphrey and Baptiste, became the pioneer gold-miners of California, and the first practical teachers of placer mining. The lumbermen around crowded in to see how they did it. The process was simple, the teachers were obliging, the lesson easy, the result sure and speedy wealth.

They soon located "claims" all about, began to hoard their "piles," and Sutter's Fort, as the place through which all new comers passed, began a rapid growth, which proved the origin and nucleus of the present capital of California.

The Sacramento of to-day stands on the east bank of the Sacramento River, about one mile below the junction of the American River, and at the head of tide navigation.

Next to San Francisco, it is the largest city in the State, having a population of twenty thousand.

It owes its importance chiefly to four things:

1st. Its central position, in the midst of the finest agricultural region of the State.

2d. Its situation at the head of tide water on the largest river of the State.

3d. It is the great railroad centre. Four leading roads terminate there.

4th. It is the political capital, having become so in 1854.

The city was originally built on ground so low and level that the heavy floods have twice broken through the levee and nearly destroyed the town.

The two great floods were those of 1851-2 and 1861-2. Thus, by sheer necessity of self-preservation, the inhabitants have been compelled to raise the grade of all the streets, and, in fact, of almost the whole city, nearly ten feet above the original level.

Sacramento has fine schools and churches, while the gardens, and shrubbery about the houses, combined with the trees along the streets, give it a most refreshing, home-like, and attractive appearance. Beyond the depots, immense foundries and machine shops of the Central Pacific railroad, the city presents the single great attraction of the

STATE CAPITOL, an immense building occupying the centre of four blocks, bounded by L and N streets on the north and south, and by Twelfth and Tenth streets on the east and west. These four blocks were a gift from the city to the State. The building faces west, fronting three hundred and twenty feet on Tenth street, while its two wings run back along L and N streets, one hundred and sixty-four feet upon each. Its height is eighty feet, divided into three lofty stories. The lower story is granite; those above, brick. The main entrance is approached by granite steps, twenty-five feet high and eighty feet wide. The style of architecture is composite—the Roman Corinthian. The building was begun ten years ago, has been steadily carried on since, and will probably require two or three years longer for its full completion.

The Interior.—Entering the vestibule, we find ourselves in a hall twenty feet deep, seventy-three feet wide, and having broad stairs on either hand. From the vestibule a broad and high-arched doorway, admits us to the

Rotunda, seventy-two feet in diameter, and rising through the height of the first dome. In the wall, between the openings of the different broad halls, are four niches to be filled by statues of Washington, Lincoln, a pioneer miner, and a pioneer hunter, one half larger than life. Above these niches and the hall entrances, will be eight panels, each thirteen feet by six, with stucco frames for frescoes. Directly over each of these will be a round panel for similar purposes, and with similar ornamentation. Above these circular panels, will be a row of thirteen sunken panels, each thirteen by eight and a half feet, to be filled with pictures; and over these, still higher up, a tier of frames, each ten by sixteen feet, numbering sixteen in all, and also intended for paintings. The frames of these last extend clear to the bottom of the sky-light, and are to be painted red, white and blue, successively, thus presenting from below a huge sixteen pointed star of the national colors.

The First Story is twenty-one and a half feet high. From the right of the rotunda, a hall sixteen feet wide, leads south through the centre of that wing. First, on the right, are the Secretary of

State's two rooms, twenty-nine feet wide, and having a united length of forty-seven feet, elegantly finished and furnished. Beyond these, in the southwest corner, is a reception, or committee room, twenty-seven by thirty, while the other corner has a like space divided into two rooms for similar purposes. Opposite the Secretary's is the Chief Justice's room. As we may not have time to descend to and describe the lower or ground floor, we may here say that its space is mainly occupied by the Judges of the Supreme Court. In the north wing we have a similar arrangement of rooms, and to be occupied by the State Treasurer, Controller, Attorney-General, Board of Education, besides two yet unassigned.

Returning to the rotunda, and going east, we enter the

Supreme Court Room, occupying a circular or ellipsoidal projection built out from the east side of the building between the two wings. The room is fifty-eight by forty-six feet, lofty and well-lighted. Thence, crossing a hall on the southwest, one enters the Supreme Court Library Room, twenty-eight by thirty-three feet, and containing four thousand volumes.

The Second Floor has a height of twenty feet clear, with halls like those below. Along the central portion of the main hall the rooms on either side are the Public Law Library Room, two Committee rooms on each side of the Library, two rooms for the Sergeants-at-Arms of the Assembly and the Senate, and eight Committee Rooms. Occupying the east half of the south wing is the Senate chamber, while the Assembly chamber has the corresponding location in the north wing, and the State Library occupies the circular projection on the east side immediately over the Supreme Court Room already described. Between the

Senate Chamber and the hall swing a pair of magnificent double doors of solid black walnut, inclosing beautiful panels of California laurel-wood, bordered by elaborate carving. These doors are thirteen feet high by seven feet wide, and six inches thick, and for massive elegance and costliness, are among the noticeable features of the Capitol. The Chamber itself is sixty-two feet deep, seventy-two feet wide, and forty-six feet high.. A continuous gallery, supported by eight Corinthian columns, extends across the west side, and throws a wing some distance forward on both the north and south. These columns are copied from those in portico of Septimus Severus at Rome. Twenty windows light the room by day, and two large gilt and crystal chandeliers by night. The President's desk occupies a recess in the centre of the east side. Above the desk, large gold letters present the motto, " Senatoris est civitatis libertatem tueri." A full-length portrait of Washington hangs above this motto. The senators' desks are of black walnut, of large size, and handsome pattern. A capacious arm-chair, upholstered with crimson plush velvet, accompanies each desk.

The Assembly Chamber occupies the eastern portion of the north wing. It measures ten feet more each way than the Senate Chamber; has the same style of architecture, and closely resembles that room in its general finish and furnishing, except that the desks and chairs are twice as numerous; the senators numbering forty, the assemblymen, eighty. The upholstering of the chairs of this room is of green velvet. Very rich and heavy carpets of elegant patterns cover the floors of both rooms. The motto of this hall is, "Legislatorum est justas leges condere." Over the motto hangs a life-size portrait of General Sutter, the founder of the city. Still above the portrait, in a sort of arched niche, is a statue of Minerva, having a horn of plenty on her right and a California bear upon her left. A like statue similarly flanked, occupies the corresponding position in the Senate Chamber.

The State Library.—The State Library occupies the circular or elipsoidal projection midway between the north and south wings on the east side of the building, immediately over the Supreme Court rooms. The Library Room is fifty-eight feet long by forty-six feet wide, and forty-six feet high. Its plan is unique. In the centre, a rotunda, rising straight up through, is crowned by a dome, whose top is sixty-three feet above the floor. A broad, circular gallery divides the room into two stories, each of which is itself again divided into two by a sub-gallery. The circular space around the rotunda, contains nine equal alcoves. The peculiar outline produces a singular, and somewhat startling effect, which is, that when standing in the centre of this library, one cannot see a single book, although the shelves around him contain nearly thirty thousand volumes. Convenient stairs give easy access to galleries and sub-galleries; all of which are arranged in the same manner. Counting the different levels from which ascend the successive tiers of radial shelving, the library room is four stories high. The dome rests on twelve Corinthian columns, similar to those in the Senate and Assembly chambers, already described. Still above the library, surrounding the rotunda, is a large circular room, devoted to the storage of papers, pamphlets, and congressional reports.

The Third Floor is eighteen feet high in the clear, and is divided into seventeen committee rooms, besides a large hall in the southwest corner of the south wing, which is provided for a cabinet and museum.

The Dome.—Over the inner dome, already built, will be erected the main or outer dome, one hundred feet higher, supported on massive iron columns, and surmounted by Powers' statue of California, in iron.

The Grounds about the building, covering the four blocks donated by the city, will be terraced and sodded, set with native trees, beautiful flower plots, traversed by graveled walks, inclosed by a massive and costly fence, and entered by gateways at the corners and at the centres of each side.

Over $1,000,000, in gold coin, has already been expended upon it, and it is more than probable that the better part of another million will follow the first, before Californians will witness the completion of their costly capitol, which is, however, as it should be, by far the noblest building west of the Mississippi.

Although still unfinished, the Legislature took formal possession of the building on Monday, Dec. 6th, 1869. The Secretary of State, State Treasurer, Supreme Judges, and several other State officials, already occupy the apartments assigned to them.

OTHER BUILDINGS.—The new Odd Fellows' Hall, the Savings Bank Building, two or three of the churches, the residence of Chas. Crocker, and those of several other prominent gentlemen, equal the finest in the State.

HOTELS.—The Golden Eagle and the Orleans are the best. The former is newer, stands nearer the Capitol, and accommodates the legislators. The latter is newly and elegantly furnished and is the great haunt of the railroad men. As for tables and beds, either will furnish you the best in the city. Each runs free coaches from the depots and wharves.

VIEW OF THE CITY.—No neighboring natural eminence affords any point of sight worth noting. From the Capitol dome, however, one has a view of the tree-embowered city, and the far-reaching, fertile valley, the gracefully winding, tree-bordered river, and the distant, snow-capped mountains, which form a panorama of beauty, shut in by grandeur, rarely to be enjoyed from as slight an elevation.

Stockton.

A trifle over one third of the way down from Sacramento to San Francisco, lies Stockton, the county seat of San Joaquin County, and in population, the fourth city of the State. It stands on both banks of a deep and wide slough of the same name, navigable the year round, and opening into the San Joaquin river, three miles west of the city. It was named in compliment to Commodore Stockton, in honorable recognition of his prominent services in the conquest of the State.

No city in California has had a more gradual, steady and healthful growth. For many years it was the point of departure and the centre of trade for several of the richest mining regions, of which business it still retains, directly or indirectly, a full proportion. Its great source of prosperity and of wealth, however, is the immense grain-producing country, the famous San Joaquin valley, which surrounds it.

Last year, 1870, Stockton exported 94,152,000 lbs., nearly 50,000 tons, of wheat; and 3,160,500 lbs. of wool; 53,586 tons of hay, and nearly 160 tons of butter and cheese.

THE ARTESIAN WELL.—One of the points of vital interest to the inhabitants, if not to every tourist, is the great well, one thousand and two feet deep, seven inches in diameter, and discharging three hundred and sixty thousand gallons daily.

THE INSANE ASYLUM.—The chief architectural attractions of Stockton are the two large and fine buildings of the State Insane Asylum, occupying most extensive, beautifully planned, and tastefully kept grounds, in the northern part of the city. The institution was opened in 1853, and has now about eleven hundred patients in care. It is the most expensive public institution yet completed in the State, having cost nearly one million dollars. It is open to visitors at stated hours, except the female department, through which gentlemen are not allowed to pass, unless by special permission of, or in company with, the attendant physician. Superintendent and Resident Physician, Dr. G. A. Shurtleff.

HOTELS.—Of the six or eight hotels in the city, only two rank as first-class. The Yosemite House is emphatically *the* tourist's home. The moment you step upon the depot platform, or the steamboat pier, look out for the bluest eye, the fairest hair, and the most attractive face in the crowd, and ride home with their owner. He's one of the three McBean brothers, whose excellent management has made the Yosemite House so widely known and so increasingly popular. The Grand Hotel is the other first-class house, and is conducted upon the restaurant plan.

ROUTES AND TEAMS.—If you want to know where to go and how to get there, ask for Robert C. Patten, or address him through box 91, Stockton P. O., and he'll make any desired arrangements for you, in the kindest way, the promptest time, and at the lowest rate.

From Stockton toward Oakland.

The Western Pacific railroad takes us first, to

Lathrop,

Nine miles west of Stockton. Here is the junction of the Visalia division of the Central Pacific railroad now open to

Modesto,

Twenty-one miles south, on the Tuolumne river. This is one of the present points of departure for the

Calaveras Big Trees and the Yosemite Valley, whither stages depart daily.

Returning to Lathrop and continuing west about one mile thence, we cross the

San Joaquin River,

Broad, shallow and muddy, bordered by level reaches of tule lands, so low that a few feet rise in the river overflows thousands of acres, and makes the river sometimes nearly six miles wide. A necessity, resulting from this overflow, is the San Joaquin Bridge, which not only spans the permanent bed of the roily stream, but extends several miles across the low tule lands, whose submergence would otherwise completely stop all travel, except by swimming, wading, boating or flying.

Seven miles from Lathrop, we come to

Banta's,

A small freight and passenger station, whence tri-weekly stages connect for Hill's Ferry, forty miles.

Five miles further, through a fine agricultural country, brings us to

Ellis,

A small village clustered round the usual saloons and restaurants; whence six miles more and we reach

Midway,

Whose name will never be true till either San Francisco or Sacramento moves six miles nearer the other.

Seven and a half miles further, we suddenly plunge into a well-cut tunnel, about six hundred feet long, whose chief peculiarity is that we enter it in one county and leave it in another. It receives us in San Joaquin county, carries us under the boundary, and ushers us into Alameda county. Just after coming out from the tunnel, we whirl by the little flag station Altamont, whence we begin to enter upon the down grade, and roll through the

Livermore Pass,

Which is either a valley or a hill, according to whether one reckons downward from the higher summits on either side, or upward from the lower level at either end. Eight miles from Altamont we stop at

Livermore,

A rapidly-growing village in the beautiful Livermore Valley, forty-seven miles from San Francisco. From this station down to

Pleasanton,

Is only six miles, and they are *pleasant 'uns* indeed.

A thriving town, finely situated and beautifully surrounded.

Thence rolling rapidly down the tortuous track, we skirt along the bases of high hills, follow the windings of a charming little narrow valley, rumbling through two or three strong frame bridges, for twelve miles, when

Niles,

And its junction, with " change cars for San José," notify us that we have fairly passed the hills, and entered upon the fertile plains which gently slope from the foothills to the bay, whose southern portion is our first glimpse of Pacific salt water. At Niles we can take the San José cars, and go round, through that city, to San Francisco, all the way by land, if we particularly desire to accomplish the whole transit on wheels. If we do that, we shall travel forty miles further than by keeping straight on from Niles through

Decoto,

which is but two miles. Decoto is one of the "going to be" towns. At present it exists chiefly in the future tense. Nine miles still between the rolling foothills on the right and the almost level plains stretching away bayward, brings us to

San Lorenzo,

Which presents nothing of special note beyond a quiet, restful-looking town, quite refreshing to the tired and dusty tourist. Thence four miles, and

San Leandro,

Town and creek, arrest our train for sixty seconds, The court house, jail, a large agricultural implement factory, with several stores, one or two hotels and a newspaper, invest this pleasant town with all the dignity of a comfortable county seat. Seven miles from San Leandro, is

Brooklyn,

A thriving, go-ahead town of two thousand inhabitants nights, and about seventeen hundred by day, when a good seventh of its denizens are away at their business in San Francisco. Thence a short two miles, and we stop again at

Oakland,

The tree-embowered city named by nature, and chosen by man for charming homes and quiet halls of learning.

Moving once more, and for the last time, we steam by the hedges, gardens, cottages and mansions along the southwest suburb, and roll slowly out two miles along a strongly built pier, over the shallow margin of the bay, or the undisguised flats, according to the tide, and " down brakes" for good on the last rails of the great iron way across the continent, and over the waters of another ocean. An elegant ferry-boat, "El Capitan," quickly receives us, and, in fifteen minutes, the San Francisco pier welcomes us to the Occidental metropolis, and our journey is done. Turn, now, to the paragraph on hacks and hotels; let one take you to the other, bathe, eat and sleep, and next morning, hunt up the " Short Excursions in and about San Francisco," and devote yourself to cultivating the Pacific metropolis.

Lake Tahoe.

This beautiful mountain lake lies along the eastern margins of Placer and El Dorado counties. The State line between California and Nevada passes through it, lengthwise, from north to south. We reach it by stage from the Central Pacific railroad at Truckee, in three hours, over a variable road, through scenery often beautiful, and for the extravagant fare of $3.00.

The lake is one mile and a quarter above the sea level. It is itself a little inland sea, thirty miles long, from eight to fifteen wide, and in places nearly two thousand feet deep. Its water is clear as crystal, cold as the melting ice and snows which feed it, and the purest known upon the continent.

Floating upon its surface, and looking down through its water, one can easily count the pebbles and stones along its gravelly bottom at the depth of sixty feet. One seems suspended between two firmaments of ether, with birds flying above and fish swimming below. And such trout! swimming forty feet beneath you, and plainly visible in all their quick and graceful motions between you and the rocky bottom.

From the water's edge, grassy slopes, pebbly beaches, rocky shores and precipitous bluffs lead the eye up through tree-dotted ravines, over forest-crowned hills to snow-clad mountains, white-headed with age, and ermine-mantled upon their tremendous shoulders.

A small steamer or two ply upon the lake— plenty of good boats await one, and excellent hotels accommodate transient guests, or more permanent boarders.

From Tahoe, back to Truckee, by stage, cross the railroad, and ride out two miles to

Donner Lake,

Smaller, but hardly less beautiful than that just left. Its great beauty in itself, the wild and romantic surrounding scenery, its ease of access and its good hotel, make it a popular summer resort. The tragical circumstances, seldom equaled in the pioneer history of any country, which gave the name to this lake, may be found graphically narrated in the "Overland Monthly" for July, 1870.

If you visit these charming lakes on your journey to the State you could not have a grander introduction to its scenes of wonder and beauty ; if you take them on your return east, you could not possibly carry away more delicious memories of lovelier spots. Whether they bid you "welcome" or "farewell," you will leave them with regret, recall them with delight, and long to return and linger among their matchless charms.

COMPLETE INDEX.

ABBREVIATIONS.—S. F. San Francisco. Sac. Sacramento. S. J. San José. St. Stockton. Yo. Yosemite.

	PAGE.
Alabaster Cave	77
Alameda	196
" Ferry	196
Alcatraz Island	196–206
Alhambra Theatre, S. F.	123
Almaden Mine	214
Alta California Bldg., S.F.	157
Alvarado	211
American Ex. Hotel, S. F.	120
Angel Island	196–207
Approaches to S. F.	107
Art Gallery	133
Artesian Well, St	244
Asylums, S. F.	167–8
Auzerais House, S. J.	213
Baggage Express, S. F.	115
Bancroft's	157–172–174
Bank of Cal., S. F.	154
Banta's	246
Baseball Grounds	130
Baths	122
Bay Trips	205
Bay View Road—Track—House	147–192
Beer Cellars	124
Beet Sugar Works	211
Belmont	224
Bernal Heights, S. F.	183

	PAGE.
Big Trees	57
Billiards, S. F.	127
Black Diamond Coal Co. Mine	189–230
Black Point	196
Bonita Point	195
Bower Cave	72
Bowling Saloons, S. F.	127
Bridal Veil Fall, Yo.	28
Brief Trips, S. F.	197
Broderick Mt.	40
Brooklyn	249
Brooklyn Hotel, S. F.	120
Business Buildings and Blocks, S. F.	157–159
Butchertown	192
Calaveras Big Trees	52
Central P. R. R. Co.	190
California Street, S. F.	143
" " Hill, S.F.	181
California Theatre	123
Capitol, Sac.	236
Cathedral Rocks	30
" Spires	30
Chinese Quarter, S. F.	197
" Theatres	123
Churches, S. F.	161
Circuit of S. F.	189

	PAGE.		PAGE.
City Gardens	140	Footing it	187
City and Co. Buildings, S. F.	150–153	Fort Point	194
Clay Street Hill	180	Frogtown	219
Clayton	227	Gardens, S. F.	130
Cliff House—Road	145–199	Gas Works, S. F.	190
Cloud's Rest	41	Gilroy	215
Colleges, S. F.	169–171	Glacier Rock	33
Congress Springs	215	Glass Works	191
Conveyances, S. F.	113	Goat Island	207
Corporation Buildings, S. F.	153–157	Gold, Discovery of	233
Cosmopolitan Hotel, S.F.	119	Golden Gate	195
Court House, S. J.	213	Grand Hotel	117
Cricket Grounds, S. F.	130	Gymnasiums, S. F.	128
Crystal Chapel	85	Half Dome	41
" Springs	223	Halls, S. F.	125
Custom House, S. F.	149	Harpending's Block	157
		Hayward's	211
Dance Halls, S. F.	124	Horse Cars, S. F.	184
Dashaways	126	Hospitals, S. F.	167–190
Davenport's Landing	219	Hotels, S. F.	116
Deaf and Dumb Asylum, Berkeley	210	How to get about	184
Decoto	248	Hunter's Point	192
Deep Cut, S. F.	191	Illilouette Fall	35
Denman School	171	Industrial School	152
Donner Lake	252	Italian Fishing Fleet	191
Donohoe Building	157		
Drives, S. F.	145	Jail, S. F.	151
Dry Dock	192		
Dungeon of Enchantment	82	Kachoomah Fall	38
		Kimball Car Manufactory.	159
El Capitan	48	Lagoon, The	193
Ellis	246	Laguna Creek	218
Engine Houses, S. F.	152	Lake Honda	193
Excursion Routes	205	Lake Merced	193
		Lathrop	275
Farrallones	194	Libraries, S. F.	148
Ferries	196	Light House, Fort Point	193
Fire Department, S. F.	153	Lime Point	195
Fissure, The, Yo.	31	Lincoln School	171

INDEX.   255

	PAGE.
Livermore	247
Livery Stables	187
Lodging-houses, S. F.	121
Lone Mountain	181
Long Bridge, S. F.	191
Lumber Yards, S. F.	189
Maguire's Opera House	123
Manufactories, S. F.	159–161
Marine Hospital	150
Mariposa Big Trees	57
Marshall, Jas. W.	232
Martinez	226
Masonic Temple, S. F.	156
Mechanics' Institute	158
" Pavilion	155
Melodeons, S. F.	124
Menageries	140
Menlo Park	225
Mercantile Library, S. F.	154
Merchants' Exchange	154
Metropolitan Theatre, S.F.	123
Midway	247
Milbrae	225
Mint	149
Mirror Lake	42
Mission Bay—Peaks—Rocks	182–190
Modesto	245
Monterey	217
Mountain Lake	195
Mt. Broderick	40
Mt. Diablo	226–227
Mt. Starr King	40
Museums, S. F.	124
Nevada Fall	38
New Almaden	214
New York Exchange Hotel, S. J.	213
Niles	248
North Beach	196

	PAGE.
North Dome	43
" Point	196
Oakland	209–249
" Ferry	196
Ocean House—Road	146–193
" Race Course	193
Odd Fellows' Hall, S. F.	156
Pacheco	226
Pacific Bank, S. F.	193
P. M. S. S. Co.	196
Pacific Rolling Mill	160 191
Pajaro Valley	216
Palace Car	159
Parks, S. F.	130
Pescadero	220
" Creek	222
Pigeon Point	219
Pioneers, Society of	153
Pioneer Woolen Mills	196
Pleasanton	247
Point Bonita	195
" Lobos	194
Points of Observation	174
Pompompasus	47
Post-office, S. F.	148
Potrero	191
Presidio	195
Private Residences, S. F.	174
Promenades, S. F.	141–144
Pulpit, The	87
Redwood City	224
Restaurants, S. F.	121
Rincon Hill	181
" Point	190
Rope Walk, S. F.	191
Royal Arches, Yo.	44
Russian Hill	180
Sacramento	231–2
San Bruno Road	192

	PAGE.
SAN FRANCISCO	95-204
Approaches	107
Baths	122
Buildings—Business	157
" Public	148
Chinese Quarter	197
Churches	161
Colleges	169
Conveyances	113
Drives	145
Excursions about City	197
Gymnasiums	128
Halls	125
Hills	174
Historical Sketch	95
Horse Cars	184
Hospitals, Asylums, etc.	167
Hotels	116
How to get about	184
Libraries	148
Lodging Houses	121
Manufactories	159
Melodeons	124
Museums	124
Places of Amusement	122
Plan of City	102
Private Residences	174
Promenades	141
Restaurants	121
Schools	171
Sea Wall	196
Situation and Extent	99
Skating Rinks	130
Squares and Parks	141
Suburbs and Vicinity	188
Theatres	122
San Joaquin River	246
San José—Trip	212
San Juan	217
San Leandro	249
San Lorenzo	249
San Mateo	223

	PAGE.
San Quentin	196
Santa Clara	215
Santa Cruz	217
Saratoga	215
Saucelito	196
Scott's Creek	219
Sea Wall	196
Seal Rocks	194
Sentinel Dome	32
Sentinel Rock	31
Ship Yards, S. F.	161
Shot Tower, S. F.	161
Skating Rinks, S. F.	130
South San Francisco	192
State Normal School, S.J.	213
State University	210
Sugar Refineries	161
Sutter, Gen. Jno. A.	232
Tahoe, Lake	250
Telegraph Hill	174
Tenaya Cañon	41
" Lake	43
Three Brothers	47
Tooloolweack Fall	36
Tutochahnulah	48
Vallejo	196
Vernal Fall	35
Visitacion Point and Val.	192
Waddell's Wharf	219
Warm Springs	211
Washington Column	44
Woodward's Gardens	130-140
YOSEMITE	24-48
For Routes, Conveyances, Time, Hotels, Guides, Horses, Outfit, and Expenses see	
Introduction	

INDEX TO ADVERTISERS.

BIG TREES, Calaveras Co.,
  Sperry & Perry, - - xliii
CENTRAL PAC. R. R.
  Yosemite route - - xv
GEYSERS.
  Great Geyser Springs, J. C. Susenbeth - - - xvi
GILROY.
  Hanna House, J. A. Gordon & Co., - - - xliv
MODESTO.
  Ross House, J. Cole - xvii
NAPA CITY.
  Revere House, J.W. Sharp xviii
OAKLAND.
  Taylor's Carpet Store, - liii
PETALUMA.
  American Hotel Mrs. Wm. Ordway - - - xix
SAN FRANCISCO.
  A. L. Bancroft & Company, Books and Stationery Cover
  A. L. Bancroft & Company, Pianos - - - - vii
  Blake, Robbins & Co., Paper - - - - - xii
  Bradley & Rulofson, Photographs - - - - xx
  California Ink Company, G. L. Faulkner - - - xxi
  City Livery and Sale Stables, M. Magner, - - xlv
  Eagle Pencils - xxii
  R. Eitner, Engraver, xxiii
  Jos Figel, Merchant Tailor xxiv
  L P. Fisher, Advertising Agent - - - xxv

  Grand Hotel, Johnson & Co xlvi
  Henry G. Hanks, Assayer and Chemist - - - lvi
  Hobbs, Gilmore & Co. - xxvi
  J. Isaac & Co., stationery xi
  Sam'l Kellett, Plaster, Decorations, - - - xlviii
  McAfee, Spiers & Co., Boiler Makers - - - viii
  J. C. Meussdorffer, Hats xxvii
  New York Livery Stable, Crittenden & Dalton - xlix
  Occidental Hotel, - xxviii
  Overland Monthly, J. H. Carmany & Co. - - vi
  Geo. T. Pracy - xxix
  H. Rosekrans & Co., Hardware - - - xxx
  Sherman & Hyde, Music Dealers - - xxxi
  Thurnauer & Zinn, Willowware - - - xxxii
  Watkins' Photographic Views, - - - - - xiii
  Woodward's Gardens - lvii

SAN JOSE.
  Auzerais House - l
  Church & Wallace, Teams and Saddle Horses - lvi
  New York Exchange Hotel li

STOCKTON.
  Yosemite House - - liv

YOSEMITE.
  Coulterville route - xxxiii
  Coulterville and Mariposa route, C. P. R. R. - xv
  New Yosemite Hotel, Leidig & Davaney, - - lii

INDEX TO ADVERTISERS.

BOSTON.
   And. T. Graves, Books - xxxiv
   Henry Hoyt, New Prize Books
      - - - - xxxv
   Lee & Shepard, Schwartz Novels - - - - xiv
   Lee & Shepard, Books of Travel - - - xxxvi
   Loring's R. R. Novels - lv
   H. A. Young & Co., Books xxxvii

NEW YORK.
   Appleton's Guide Books xxxviii
   Eagle Pencils - - xxii
   Gillott's Pens   Inside Cover
   Harper's Periodicals, - iii
   J. S. Redfield, Books - xxxix
   S. R. Wells, Phrenology xl
   Shipmans' Patent File - v
   Spencerian Pens, Ivison, Blakeman & Taylor - - iv

PALMYRA. N. Y.
   Globe Printing Presses - x

PHILADELPHIA.
   Chas. Desilver, School Books - - - - . - xli
   Kay & Brother, Publishers, &c. - - - xlii

SPRINGFIELD, MASS.
   Webster's Dictionaries ix

Harper's Periodicals.

HARPER'S MAGAZINE.

The great design of *Harper's* is to give correct information and rational amusement to the great masses of the people. There is no monthly Magazine an intelligent reading family can less afford to be without. Many Magazines are accumulated. *Harper's* is edited.—*New England Homestead.*

HARPER'S WEEKLY.

The best publication of its class in America, and so far ahead of all other weekly journals as not to permit of any comparison between it and any of their number.—*Boston Traveler.*
Harper's Weekly is the best and most interesting illustrated newspaper. Nor does its value depend on its illustrations alone. Its reading-matter is of a high order of literary merit—varied, instructive, entertaining, and unexceptionable.—*N. Y. Sun.*

HARPER'S BAZAR.

Free from all political and sectarian discussion, devoted to fashion, pleasure, and instruction, it is just the agreeable, companionable, and interesting domestic paper which every mother and wife and sweetheart will require every son, husband, and lover to bring home with him, every Saturday evening.—*Philadelphia Ledger.*

TERMS:

HARPER'S MAGAZINE, One Year,....................$4 00
HARPER'S WEEKLY, One Year,.................... 4 00
HARPER'S BAZAR, One Year,.................... 4 00

HARPER'S MAGAZINE, HARPER'S WEEKLY, and HARPER'S BAZAR, to one address, for one year, $10 00; or any two for $7 00.

An extra copy of either the MAGAZINE, WEEKLY, or BAZAR will be supplied gratis for every club of FIVE SUBSCRIBERS at $4 00 each, in one remittance; or Six Copies for $20 00, without extra copy.

SPENCERIAN
STEEL PENS.

Manufactured by the Original Inventor of Steel Pens.

The celebrated durability and perfection of action of these Pens are owing to a peculiar process of Carbonizing and to the great care taken in their manufacture by the most skilled and experienced workmen in Europe. They are a nearer approximation to the real SWAN QUILL than anything hitherto invented.

For Sale by Dealers generally.

☞ SAMPLE CARD. containing all the 14 NUMBERS artistically arranged and securely enclosed, sent by mail on receipt of 25 CENTS.

The Traveler's Vade Mecum.
Lately Published.

A Pocket Dictionary of the English Language.

Abridged from Webster's Quarto, illustrated with nearly TWO HUNDRED Engravings on Wood. By Wm. G. Webster, and Wm. A. Wheeler.

THE ILLUSTRATED CATALOGUE, descriptive of The American Educational Series of School and College Text-Books, and THE EDUCATIONAL REPORTER, a handsome publication full of useful information, mailed free to any address.

Ivison, Blakeman, Taylor & Co.,
PUBLISHERS,
138 and 140 Grand Street, New York.

FOR SAVING VALUABLE PAPERS
NOTHING EQUALS
SHIPMAN'S
PATENT ADHESIVE
Letter and Invoice File.

We would respectfully call the attention of Business Men, Bankers and others, to our Patent Adhesive Letter and Invoice File.

We claim that it is the best article in use for the preservation of all kinds of printed or written documents, such as Letters, Invoices, Bills, &c. &c. They are in use by most of the Business Firms and Companies in the United States.

Its form is that of a *scrap book*, of various sizes, having narrow leaves with adhesive surface, which requires only to be moistened and the document applied; thus it becomes a *book* of 250 or 500 letters, *arranged* in the order of *dates*, secure from *loss* or *misplacement*, and as convenient for *reference* as a ledger account—and this with the least expense of time. Every lover of order or economist of time must appreciate its importance.

We also keep constantly on hand, in great variety, Invoice and Scrap Books, Letter Copying Books, Blank Books and a full assortment of Stationery.

ASA L. SHIPMAN & SONS,
25 Chambers Street, New York.

SUBSCRIBE FOR THE

Overland Monthly

The only Literary Magazine

PUBLISHED ON THE PACIFIC COAST.

The Seventh Volume of this popular California Magazine will commence with the July Number for 1871. Its popularity has induced the publishers to make still greater exertions in producing an interesting and instructive periodical.

TERMS:—$4.00 per annum, *payable in advance*.

CLUB RATES:—Two copies, $7.00; Five copies, $16.00; Ten copies, $30.00; and each additional copy, $3.00. For every Club of Twenty Subscribers, an extra copy will be furnished GRATIS.

PUBLISHED BY

JOHN H. CARMANY & CO.
No. 409 WASHINGTON STREET
SAN FRANCISCO.

PIANOS, ORGANS,

AND

MUSIC PUBLICATIONS.

NEW PIANO AGENCY.—Messrs. A. L. Bancroft & Co. have organized, under the management of Wm. Henry Knight, a MUSIC DEPARTMENT, where may be found a complete assortment of PIANOS, ORGANS, SHEET MUSIC AND MUSIC PUBLICATIONS. Following are some of their specialties:

I. The GEORGI PIANO-FORTE—a new and magnificent instrument; in every respect strictly first-class, and becoming very popular in the East.

II. The PRINCE ORGANS AND MELODEONS.— There are 46,500 of these now in use. They are unsurpassed among reed organs.

III. The McCAMMON PIANOS, formerly known as the celebrated "Boardman & Gray" Piano. A very superior, moderate priced instrument.

IV. The COTTAGE AND SCHOOL PIANO.—In small sized cases, elegant in appearance, of low cost, and very durable.

V. HOOK'S PIPE ORGANS FOR CHURCHES.—The best manufactured.

VI. LUNAN'S GERMAN UPRIGHT PIANOS.—Fine-toned, thoroughly well made instruments.

VII. MUSIC PUBLICATIONS.—Sheet Music, Instruction Books, etc., etc.

For Descriptive Circulars and Price Lists, address or apply to

A. L. BANCROFT & COMPANY,
Music Department,
Bancroft's Building, SAN FRANCISCO.

McAfee, Spiers & Co.,

Boiler Makers and GENERAL MACHINISTS.

High and Low-Pressure Boilers,

STATIONARY AND MARINE.

Howard St., bet. Fremont and Beale,

SAN FRANCISCO.

Also Orders received for every description of Machinery.

Having 24 years' experience in this business, we feel confident of being able to compete, as to quality of work, with any establishment on the Pacific Coast.

Particular and personal attention given to repairs of old boilers on steamships and steamboats.

GET THE BEST
Webster's Unabridged
DICTIONARY.

10,000 Words and Meanings not in other Dictionaries. 3,000 Engravings. 1,840 Pages Quarto. Price $12.

Glad to add my testimony in its favor.
[President Walker of Hartford.]

Every scholar knows its value.
[W. H. Prescott, the Historian.]

The most complete Dictionary of the Language.
[Dr. Dick, of Scotland.]

The best guide of students of our language.
[John G. Whittier.]

He will transmit his name to latest posterity.
[Chancellor Kent.]

Etymological parts surpasses anything by earlier laborers.
[George Bancroft.]

Bearing relation to Language Principia does to Philosophy.
[Elihu Burritt.]

Excels all others in defining scientific terms.
[President Hitchcock.]

So far as I know, best defining Dictionary.
[Horace Mann.]

Take it altogether, the surpassing work.
[Smart, the English Orthœpist.]

A necessity for every intelligent family, student, teacher and professional man. What library is complete without the best English Dictionary?

Published by G. & C. MERRIAM, Springfield, Mass.

Sold by A. L. BANCROFT & CO., San Francisco, and all Booksellers.

Also, WEBSTER'S NATIONAL PICTORIAL DICTIONARY.

1040 Pages Octavo. 600 Engravings. Price $5.

The work is really a *gem of a Dictionary*, just the thing for the millions.— *American Educational Monthly.*

Globe Printing Presses.

IMPRESSION CAN BE THROWN OFF.
DWELL ON THE IMPRESSION.
DETENTION OF ROLLERS ON CYLINDER
AND DOUBLE VIBRATING DISTRIBUTORS,
GIVING UNLIMITED DISTRIBUTION.

NET CASH PRICES:

Half medium, 13 x 19½ inches inside of chase, $550.00. Fountain, $25.00. Steam Fixtures, $15.00. Boxing, $10.00.—extra.
Quarto medium, 10 x 15 inches inside of chase, $425.00. Fountain, $25.00. Steam Fixtures, $15.00. Boxing, $7.00.—extra.
Eighth medium, 8 x 12 inches inside of chase, $250.00. Steam Fixtures, $15.00. Boxing, $6.00.—extra.
One Roller Mould, two sets Roller Stocks, and three chases, are included with each Press.

All of these Presses will be thoroughly tested, strongly boxed, and delivered to the order of the purchaser, at our manufactory, Palmyra, N. Y.

Jones Manufacturing Co.
Palmyra, N. Y.

JOSEPH ISAAC.   H. ROBITSCHECK.

J. ISAAC & CO.,

IMPORTERS AND JOBBERS OF

Stationery, Blank Books,

MANILA AND WRAPPING PAPERS,

PLAYING CARDS, LABELS, LIQUOR ESSENCES,

ETC., ETC., ETC.

513 Sansome St., cor. Merchant

SAN FRANCISCO.

J. ISAAC & CO'S
Paper Warehouse.

DEALERS IN PAPERS

OF ALL DESCRIPTIONS,

Envelopes, Inks, Twine, Playing Cards,

LIQUOR AND WINE LABELS,

ESSENTIAL OILS, ETC., ETC.

Blake, Robbins & Co.,

IMPORTERS AND JOBBERS OF

Book, News, Writing and
WRAPPING PAPER,

Paper Bags, Card Stock, Straw Paper,

Straw and Binders' Board, Inks, Bronzes, Etc.

AGENTS FOR

Carson's Celebrated Letter Papers,

INFERIOR TO NONE.

Agents for Dexter's Manila Papers.

AGENTS FOR WHITING MILL PAPER,

AND OTHER LEADING BRANDS.

---

516 Sacramento & 519 Commercial Sts.

SAN FRANCISCO.

FRANCIS BLAKE,
JAMES MOFFITT,   } San Francisco.
CHAS. F. ROBBINS,
JAMES W. TOWNE, New York.

New York Office, 18 and 20 *Vesey Street.*

WATKINS'

YOSEMITE GALLERY,

429 MONTGOMERY STREET,

San Francisco, Cal.

Photographic Views

Of Yosemite Valley, the Big Trees, the Mines, the splendid Scenery of the

CENTRAL PACIFIC RAILROAD,

The Coast etc., etc. Can be had in all sizes for framing, the Album, or the Stereoscope.

Sold Wholesale and Retail. A liberal discount made to the trade. *You are requested to visit the Gallery.*

The Most Popular Novels
ARE THE
SCHWARTZ NOVELS.

Translated from the Swedish of MADAME MARIE SOPHIE SCHWARTZ, by MISS SELMA BORG, and MISS MARIE A. BROWN.

NOW READY.

GUILT AND INNOCENCE. Paper, $1 00; Cloth, $1 50.

"Madame Schwartz is a writer of much greater literary merit than Miss Muhlbach, whose works have been so widely circulated in this country.'"—*New York Atlas.*

GOLD AND NAME. Paper, $1 00; Cloth, $1 50.

"This is a powerful book; in plot and style, it is equally good. Its morals— it may be considered to have several—are unexceptionable."—*Christian Standard, Cincinnati.*

BIRTH AND EDUCATION. Paper. $1 00; Cloth, $1 50.

"This title would make one suppose that it was a book devoted to common schools and academies. Instead of that, it is a romance of the very highest class,—one of the best historical novels of the age."—*Albany Evening Post.*

THE WIFE OF A VAIN MAN. 8vo., Paper, $1 00; Cloth, $1 50.

In presenting to American readers the first translations of this author, who in her own country is universally popular, the publishers take pleasure in making public the following tribute of the Great Swedish Lyric Artiste, MLLE. CHRISTINE NILSSON.

NEW YORK, November 28, 1870.

MADEMOISELLE:—It is with great pleasure that I have learned that you, in conjunction with Miss MARIE A. BROWN have undertaken to translate into English the magnificent works of MADAME SCHWARTZ.

Allow me then, dear Mademoiselle, as a fervent admirer of MADAME SCHWARTZ, to offer you and Miss BROWN my liveliest felicitations for having chosen an author of so immense merit to introduce to the American public a writer who has contributed to make the glory of our country.

I wish you all the success you deserve, and beg you to be so kind as to send me a copy of the work as soon as it is published.

Accept, Mademoiselle, as well as Miss BROWN, my warmest sympathy and the assurance of my perfect consideration.

CHRISTINE NILSSON.

Sold by all booksellers and newsdealers, and sent by mail postpaid on receipt of price.

Lee & Shepard, Publishers, Boston.
Lee, Shepard & Dillingham,
47 and 49 Greene St., N. Y.

YOSEMITE
AND
BIG TREE GROVES
IN TWO DAYS.

IMPORTANT FOR TOURISTS.

NEW ROUTE FOR 1871,

VIA THE

VISALIA DIVISION of the CENTRAL PACIFIC RAILROAD,

FROM

LATHROP,

AND FROM THE TERMINUS OF THE C. P. R. R. BY STAGE, VIA

MARIPOSA AND CLARK'S OR COULTERVILLE.

☞ For further information see page 58.

THE GREAT
GEYSER SPRINGS
OF CALIFORNIA.

THESE celebrated Springs are the greatest natural curiosity in the world, and are reached by the

NAPA VALLEY ROUTE AND THE RUSSIAN RIVER VALLEY ROUTE.

For particulars of these routes, see description in body of this guide.

The Medicinal and Curative Properties of the Geyser Springs are admitted to be equal, if not superior, to Calistoga, Baden-Baden, Aix-la-Chapel, Wiesbaden, or Homburg. THE SCENERY is wild, picturesque and grand in the extreme, and finer than that of the lower Alps.

THE PLUTON, OR GREAT SULPHUR CREEK, which runs by the Geyser Hotel, is well supplied with mountain trout; and the hills abound with deer and other game.

THE HOTEL

Is a large, two-story building, with spacious verandahs surrounding it, above and below, and has been newly furnished. New steam and sulphur bath-houses have been erected, and a large stable has been built. PRIVATE TEAMS can easily and safely drive over the new road from Calistoga, and at the Geysers will find an abundance of good feed for their horses.

SADDLE HORSES

For ladies and Gentlemen, are always on hand, at reasonable prices.

A GOOD TABLE is kept at the Hotel, and the best of Liquors and Cigars will be found at the bar. The rooms are comfortable, and the beds are all new and provided with spring mattresses.

Board and lodging per day, $3; board and lodging per week, $17.50; single meals, each, $1.50. Baths, 25. Visiting the Geyser Canons, for each person, $1. Children under ten years of age, half price.

☞ Visitors are requested not to pay the Guides, as they are furnished by the Hotel, free of charge.

Fare from San Francisco to Calistoga, per steamer and cars, $3.50. Stages from there to the Geysers, $6.00 per passage.

J. C. SUSENBETH,

P. S.—For further particulars, inquire at the office of J. S. POLACK, Esq., Room No. 1, N. W. corner of Jackson and Montgomery Sts., San Francisco.

THE SHORTEST AND
BEST ROUTE TO YOSEMITE
Via Modesto.

ROSS HOUSE,   MODESTO.
JOS. COLE, Proprietor.

Tourists will find this House conducted in first-class style. Charges moderate, and every attention paid to Guests. Stages leave this House daily for Snelling's, Hornitas, Mariposa, Yosemite, and all points south.

YOSEMITE STABLES,
MODESTO, CAL.

HORSES, CARRIAGES AND SADDLE HORSES
To let on reasonable terms.

Horses boarded with the best of care, by the day or week.

Private Teams Furnished at the shortest notice; also Two Four or Six Horse Turnouts furnished for Tourists, with Concord or Kimball Carriages, with careful and experienced Drivers.

F. H. ROSS, Proprietor.

Modesto is situated at the terminus of the Visalia Division of the C. P. R. R. The Ross House, also the Yosemite Stables were built by F. H. Ross, almost exclusively for the accommodation of Tourists, and no pains will be spared to make their visit to the House, or transit to the valley comfortable and pleasant.

REVERE HOUSE

JOHN W. SHARP, Proprietor.

Second Street, opposite Court House,

NAPA CITY.

ONLY FIRST-CLASS HOUSE IN NAPA CITY.

THIS HOUSE is fitted up in superior style, and is now open for the reception of PERMANENT AND TRANSIENT GUESTS. It is built in modern style, and the rooms are large, airy and pleasant.

THE BAR is well supplied. THE TABLE shall be second to none in the State. The farming community will find at this House the best of accommodations at reasonable prices.

AMERICAN HOTEL,

Main Street, Petaluma.

MRS. WM. ORDWAY, Proprietress.

This Hotel, first-class in every particular, is the leading house in this city and one of the best hotels on the coast.

THE BUILDING is a large, three-story, fire-proof brick, situated in the center of the business part of the city, well ventilated, supplied with water and gas, perfectly arranged with a view to comfort and convenience, containing sixty three rooms, elegant parlor, pleasant reading room, first-class Bar and Billiard room, Hair Dressing Saloon and Cigar Stand.

THE ROOMS, single and en-suite, are large, with high ceilings, well ventilated and elegantly furnished.

THE TABLE is supplied with the best the market affords, prepared and served in first-class style.

A LIVERY STABLE is connected with the Hotel. Splendid carriages are furnished upon notice at the office.

OMNIBUSES convey guests to and from the Hotel to cars and steamers, free of charge.

STAGES from the city leave from this Hotel.

Tourists, visiting the city, are shown every courtesy and attention in all departments of the Hotel.

FOR THE VERY
Best Photographs,
GO TO
BRADLEY
AND
RULOFSON,

429 Montgomery Street,

SAN FRANCISCO.

CLOSED ON SUNDAYS.

THE CALIFORNIA
INK COMPANY,

405 & 407 SANSOME STREET,

SAN FRANCISCO.

GEORGE L. FAULKNER, Agent.

Are manufacturing Writing Inks of different colors, equal if not superior to those of Eastern or Foreign manufacture.

For our Black Writing Fluid, we claim:

1st.—That it will not corrode or clog the pen, but keep it always in a bright, clean condition.

2d.—That there is no sediment that can settle and impair the color.

3d.—That it flows freely from, and is of a rich, deep color as soon as it leaves the pen.

4th.—It is not affected by acids, as an acid that would remove the ink will eat up the paper.

5th.—It cannot be washed off with water.

6th.—It is a California production, and the manufacture of the same keeps thousands of dollars in the State, that have hitherto been sent abroad for Ink.

We also make a superior article of MUCILAGE that cannot be excelled for its adhesive qualities.

LIQUID LAUNDRY BLUING.—A convenient and reliable preparation, to take the place of all others hitherto used for Laundry purposes. Put up in 8 oz. bottles and gallon jars.

The attention of the trade is respectfully solicited to these manufactures. Perfect satisfaction guaranteed.

Refer, by permission, to Messrs. A. L. Bancroft & Company, who are selling large quantities of our Writing Inks and Mucilage.

CALIFORNIA INK COMPANY,

GEO. L. FAULKNER, Agent.

SATISFACTION IN ALL CASES GUARANTEED.

ASK YOUR STATIONER FOR

EAGLE PENCILS.

These pencils, which have been before the American public for several years, are rapidly growing in popularity, and are to-day MORE EXTENSIVELY USED IN THE UNITED STATES THAN ANY OTHER.

And are pronounced by all who have given them a fair trial, to be INFERIOR TO NONE manufactured, and are sold at prices materially lower than are other first-class articles.

Office Rubber-Head pencils are very much liked by business men.

Eagle Drawing pencils are recommended in the Drawing Books now in use in the State of California, and by Drawing Teachers, and others.

EAGLE DIAMOND RUBBER IS THE BEST MANUFACTURED.

SOLD BY BOOKSELLERS & STATIONERS GENERALLY.
And at Wholesale and Retail by

A. L. Bancroft & Company,

BOOKSELLERS AND STATIONERS

721 MARKET ST., SAN FRANCISCO.

RUDOLF EITNER,

DESIGNER AND ENGRAVER ON WOOD,

629 CLAY STREET,

SAN FRANCISCO.

JOS. FIGEL,

Clothier, Merchant Tailor

AND DEALER IN

Men's and Boys' Clothing,

FURNISHING GOODS, TRUNKS, &C.

211 MONTGOMERY STREET,

Russ Block, opposite Platt's Hall,

Would respectfully invite the attention of the Public to his superior Stock of Goods, feeling confident that he can suit, both in regard to Price and Quality.

A FEATURE

In his business is the particular attention paid to the manufacture of Men's and Boys' Clothing, College and Military Uniforms of every description to Order, from a large assortment of Cloths, Cassimeres, Beavers, Scotch Tweed, etc.

Elegance of Style and Perfection of Fit are in all cases guaranteed.

A visit to my Establishment will convince you of my ability to please in every respect.

JOS. FIGEL,

No. 211 Montgomery Street, San Francisco, California.

ESTABLISHED IN 1852.

L. P. FISHER'S
ADVERTISING
AGENCY.

Rooms 20 & 21 Merchants' Exchange

CALIFORNIA ST., SAN FRANCISCO.

AGENT FOR THE SACRAMENTO UNION.

"ADVERTISING IS THE OIL WHICH WISE MEN PUT IN THEIR LAMPS." —*Modern Proverb.*

GIRARD'S SECRET.

STEPHEN GIRARD, than whom no shrewder business man ever lived, used to say in his old age:

"I have always considered advertising liberally and long to be the great medium of success in business and prelude to wealth. And I have made it an invariable rule, too, to advertise in the dullest times, as well as in the busiest, long experience having taught me that money thus spent is well laid out; as by keeping my business continually before the public, it has secured many sales that I otherwise would have lost."

Advertisements and Subscriptions solicited for papers published in California and Oregon, Washington, Utah, Idaho, Montana, Colorado, Arizona and adjacent Territories; Sandwich Islands, the British Possessions, Mexican Ports, Nicaragua, Panama, Valparaiso, Japan, China, Europe, Australia, Atlantic States, etc., etc.

N. B.—FOR SALE; bound volumes of the *Sacramento Union*, from Sept 19th, 1855, to the present time; also, the *San Francisco Evening Bulletin*, in bound volumes, from the beginning of its publication to the present time.

SAN FRANCISCO MILLS.

HOBBS, GILMORE & CO.

Manufacturers of BOXES,

ALSO,

Sawing and Planing Mills,

Market, Beale and Main Sts.

SAN FRANCISCO.

San Pedro Street, near Depot, San Jose.

FOR SALE;

SPANISH CEDAR, MAHOGANY,

AND OTHER FANCY WOOD.

☞ We are now manufacturing, and will receive orders for the manufacture of different kinds of AGRICULTURAL MACHINES.

FOR FINE HATS

GO TO

J. C. Meussdorffer.

NORTH EAST CORNER

OF

Montgomery & Bush Sts.

SAN FRANCISCO.

SAN FRANCISCO MILLS.

HOBBS, GILMORE & CO.

Manufacturers of BOXES,

ALSO,

Sawing and Planing Mills,

Market, Beale and Main Sts.

SAN FRANCISCO.

San Pedro Street, near Depot, San Jose.

FOR SALE;

SPANISH CEDAR, MAHOGANY,

AND OTHER FANCY WOOD.

☞ We are now manufacturing, and will receive orders for the manufacture of different kinds of

AGRICULTURAL MACHINES.

FOR FINE HATS

GO TO

J. C. Meussdorffer.

NORTH EAST CORNER

OF

Montgomery & Bush Sts.

SAN FRANCISCO.

GEORGE T. PRACY,
MACHINE WORKS,
109 & 111 MISSION STREET,
SAN FRANCISCO.

These Works have lately been increased, by additional tools, and we are now able to turn out any kind of work, equal to and cheaper than any establishment in the State, that is to say:—

Steam Engines, Flour and Saw Mills, Quartz Machinery, Printing Presses,

AND MACHINERY MADE OF EVERY DESCRIPTION.

IMPROVED SAFETY STORE HOISTS,

Fitted with Cutting's Patent Cams, unequaled for safety, convenience and cheapness. This Hoist can be built for about half the price of any other in use. To be seen at HAWLEY & CO'S.

ALSO, MANUFACTURER AND SOLE AGENT FOR

PRACY'S CELEBRATED GOVERNOR.
TURNING LATHES, &C CONSTANTLY ON HAND.

H. ROSEKRANS.   S. READ.

H. ROSEKRANS & CO.

IMPORTERS AND DEALERS IN

HARDWARE,

Builders' Materials, Carpenters' Tools,

HOUSE-FURNISHING UTENSILS,

AND ALL KINDS OF

SHELF HARDWARE,

135 MONTGOMERY STREET

NEAR BUSH STREET,

SAN FRANCISCO.

SHERMAN & HYDE,

IMPORTERS AND DEALERS IN

SHEET MUSIC

PIANOS, ORGANS,

AND

MUSICAL MERCHANDISE OF EVERY DESCRIPTION

Corner Kearny & Sutter Streets,

SAN FRANCISCO, CAL.

Send your orders directly to us. Remember it is no more trouble or expense to send Sheet Music by Mail, one thousand miles than it is one mile.

Music Teachers, Seminaries and Dealers liberally dealt with.

Thurnauer & Zinn,

IMPORTERS OF

French and German Fancy Baskets,

ENGLISH AND AMERICAN WILLOW WARE,

TOYS, FANCY GOODS

AND YANKEE NOTIONS,

CANE AND WILLOW CHAIRS,

LADIES' WORK STANDS,

Wooden Ware, Feather Dusters, Brushes,

ETC., ETC., ETC.

533 *MARKET STREET*,

Opposite Sutter and Sansome Streets.   SAN FRANCISCO.

The shortest and best route to

YOSEMITE VALLEY.

C. P. R. R. to Modesto, thence by stage to Coulterville, Bower Cave, Pilot Peak and Crane Flat.

Leaves Modesto on Tuesday, Thursday and Saturday at 5 o'clock, A. M., arrives at Coulterville at 2 P. M.; distance 50 miles; leaving Coulterville at 4 P. M., arrive at Bower Cave, at 7 P. M. Next morning leave Bower Cave at 6 A. M., and arrive at Crane Flat at 11 A. M. Take Saddle Horse and arrive at the Hotels in the Valley, at 4 o'clock, P. M., 15 miles horseback. Returning, leave Yosemite at 7 o'clock, A. M., distance, 46 miles, arrive at Coulterville at 5 o'clock, P. M., leave Coulterville at 5 A. M., arrive at Modesto, at 4 o'clock P. M.

The above route is superior to all others, as there is less time consumed on the road, more rest, and the whole route gives finer scenery than by any other, from the fact that after you strike the foot hills, you pass along the dividing ridge between the Tuolumne and Merced rivers, to the East, the Sierra Nevada, with Castle Peak, Mount Dames, and other prominent points, to the West, is the San Joaquin, and the Coast Range; also less dust than any other route, as the route is East and West, and the north winds that are almost constantly blowing, carry the dust from you.

And as a round trip is always desirable; parties can go by Coulterville, and out *via* Big Trees and Mariposa, or *vice versa*.

By the first of June, there will be but 2½ miles horseback riding into the valley.

The nights at Bower Cave are cool and refreshing, unsurpassed on the whole route.

Through Tickets for sale at all the railroad offices, Sacramento and Lathrop.

G. W. COULTER, *Agent.*

Office at C. B. & M; R. R. R. office 214 Montg'y Street.

VALUABLE BOOKS,

For Children and Youth.

PUBLISHED BY

ANDREW F. GRAVES,

20 CORNHILL, BOSTON, MASS.

THE SUNSHINE SERIES.—By H. N. W. B. Six volumes. 18mo., $3.60
    This is an entirely new series of books, by one of the best writers of juvenile books. They are put up in a neat box, and will be found excellent for the "SABBATH SCHOOL LIBRARY."

AMY GARNETT. One vol., 16 mo. - - - - - - $1.25

LYNDA NEWTON.—By Mrs. L. J. H. Frost. 16 mo., - - - 1.50
    An excellent book, and one which will interest every one.

DAVY'S MOTTO. 16 mo., - - - - - - - - 1.25
    It is better to do well than to say well is the motto.

JOE AND THE HOWARDS; or Armed with Eyes. By Carl. 16 mo. 1.25
    It gives much valuable information in regard to insects, both on land and water, in such a manner as cannot fail to amuse children, while it is storing their minds with that which is useful for them to know.

THE RAINFORD SERIES.—By Glance Gaylord.
    Four volumes in box, - - - - - - - $6.00

THE WOODBINE SERIES.—By Mrs. Madeline Leslie. 16mo. Illustrated, - - - - - - - - - - $1.25
    This is an entire new set, by a very popular author. Other volumes will be issued from time to time. The title pages are printed in colors.

THE ARLINGTON SERIES. 4 vols., 16mo.
    Four volumes in box, - - - - - - - $5.50

THE PERCY FAMILY.—By Rev. D. C. Eddy, D. D.
    Five volumes with neat box, - - - - - - 5.00

THE CEDAR BROOK STORIES, or the Clifford Children. By Mrs. A. S. M., author of "Only a Pauper." 5 vols. 18mo.
    The five volumes handsomely illustrated in a neat box with illuminated covers, - - - - - - - - - - 3.25

CORWIN'S WEST'S SERIES.—6 vols in a box, - - - 4.50

TOURIST'S GUIDE ADVERTISER. xxxv

HAVE YOU READ THE
NEW PRIZE BOOKS.

Both Sides of the Street, ($600) $1.60
Moth and Rust, ($300) $1.60
     Fourteenth Thousand now ready.

DIGGING A GRAVE
With a Wine-Glass.
And the First Glass of Wine.

Simple texts are sometimes more effective preachers than sermons, or whole volumes of well conceived essays. Read the two stories within the covers of this book, kind reader, and if a first glass of wine tempt you, let the prayer go forth, "'Lead us not into temptation."
Beautifully illustrated. Price $1.25.

DOWN IN A SALOON;
OR
The Minister's Protege.

By the author of the new $600.00 prize book,
"BOTH SIDES OF THE STREET."

Beautifully bound in gold and black, and sent prepaid by mail. Price, $1.50
For sale by all Booksellers.

HENRY HOYT,
No. 9 Cornhill, Boston.
For sale by A. L. Bancroft & Co.

BOOKS OF TRAVEL.
Published by
LEE & SHEPARD, BOSTON.

A Readable Book on California.
THE SUNSET LAND; or, The Great Pacific Slope. By Rev. John Todd, D. D. 1 vol. 16mo. - - - - - - $1 50
The press all over the country has given this book by Dr. Todd, the warmest praise. It contains, in a small compass, just what all desire to know of California.

The "Heathen Chinee," at Home and Abroad.
WHY AND How the Chinese Emigrate, and the means they adopt for the purpose of reaching America. By Col. Russell H. Conwell. 12mo. Cloth. Illustrated. - - - - - - $1 50
"Nothing is wanting in Mr. Conwell's book for a clear apprehension of every feature of his subject."—*Christian Union.*

Our New Possessions Surveyed.
ALASKA AND ITS RESOURCES. By Wm. H. Dall, Director of the Scientific Corps of the late Western Union Telegraph Expedition. One large octavo volume, - - - - - - $7 50
This is the only complete history of our newly acquired possessions published. The narrative is one of actual experience during a three years' residence in the country.

A Graphic and Truthful History.
HISTORY OF PARAGUAY. With Notes of Personal Observations and reminiscences of diplomacy under difficulties. By Charles A. Washburn, Commissioner and Minister Resident of the United States at Asuncion, from 1861 to 1868. In two volumes. Octavo. Illustrated with Maps and Engravings. - - $7 50
"A history stranger than many works of fiction, abounding in incidents of devoted heroism, and fearful cruelty."—*Chicago Post.*

A Journalist in Europe.
OVER THE OCEAN; or, Sights and Scenes in Foreign Lands. By Curtis Guild, Editor of the "Commercial Bulletin," Boston. Crown 8vo. - - - - - - - - $2 50
"Mr. Curtis Guild has given the public a book of travel such as they may search for elsewhere in vain."—*Boston Post.*

Sold by all booksellers and newsdealers, and sent by mail postpaid, on receipt of price.

Lee & Shepard, Publishers, Boston.
LEE, SHEPARD & DILLINGHAM, N. Y.

GET THE BEST BOOKS

FOR THE CHILDREN.

Effie Wingate's Work. By Mary Dwinell Chellis,	$1.50
Dea. Sim's Prayers. By Mary Dwinell Chellis,	1.50
Pleasant Pages and Bible Pictures, 20 illustrations;	1.50
Carl Bartlett or What can I do? By D. S. Ericson, 1 vol.	1.25
Bill Drock's Investment. By Mary Dwinell Chellis, 1 vol.	1.50
The Old Doctor's Son. By Mary Dwinell Chellis,	1.50
Mr. Pendleton's Cup. By Glance Gaylord,	1.25
Miss Patience Hathaway. By Glance Gaylord,	1.50
Donald Deane. By Glance Gaylord,	1.50
Good Measure. A story for boys. By D. S. Ericson,	1.50
Clean Your Boots, Sir? A capital story for boys,	.60
The Little Peanut Merchant	1.25
Molly's Bible. By Miss Mary D. Chellis,	1.50
Truth and Trust, or Iron Mountain,	1.25
Hopes and Fears, or Broad Oaks,	1.25
Good for Evil, or Rose Cottage,	1.25
Sidney de Grey, or the Rival School Boys. By Lawrence Lancewood,	1.25
Nellie Warren, or the Lost Watch. By Lawrence Lancewood, Esq.,	1.25
Louis Sinclair. By Lawrence Lancewood, Esq.,	1.25
Mark Dunning's Enemy. By Mary Dwinell Chellis,	1.50
The Hermit of Holcombe. By Mary Dwinell Chellis,	1.50
Breaking the Rules,	1.25
Earl Whiting.	1.25
The Runaway Boy,	1.25
Nellie Milton's Housekeeping,	1.25
Brownie Sandford,	1.25
Sylvia's Burden,	1.25
Ruth Lovell,	1.25
Cousin Clara. By Lawrence Lancewood,	1.25
Jamie Noble,	1.25
Peter Clinton. By Lawrence Lancewood,	1.25
A Hole in the Pocket. By Aunt Hattie,	1.25
Stopping the Leak. By Aunt Hattie,	1.25
Lost but Found. By Aunt Hattie,	1.25
Fashion and Folly. By Aunt Hattie,	1.25
Gypsy Breynton. By Miss E. Stuart Phelps.	1.25
Gypsy's Cousin Joy. By Miss E Stuart Phelps,	1.25
Gypsy's Sowing and Reaping. By Miss E. Stuart Phelps,	1.25
Gypsy's Year at the Golden Crescent, By Miss E. Stuart Phelps,	1.25

PUBLISHED BY

HENRY A. YOUNG & CO.,

GUIDE BOOKS
FOR TRAVELERS,

PUBLISHED BY

D. APPLETON & COMPANY.

APPLETONS' EUROPEAN GUIDE BOOK.—Including England, Scotland and Ireland, France, Belgium, Holland, Northern and Southern Germany, Switzerland, Italy, Spain and Portugal, Russia, Denmark, Norway and Sweden. Containing a Map of Europe, and Nine other Maps, with Plans of 20 of the Principal Cities, and more than 120 Engravings. One vol., thick 12mo, morocco, tuck, gilt edges. $6.00

"This is a curious, a useful and an interesting book—a veritable directory of travel, of immense value to the American tourists visiting the Old World for the first time, and to the native of Britain newly exploring the Continent."—*London Examiner and Review.*

"'Appletons' European Guide Book' is a compact manual for the foreign traveler, crowding a great variety of information into a small compass, by a rigorous brevity of statement, and the omission of all irrelevant details.—*New York Tribune.*

"'Appletons' Guide' is likely to create a stir among those with which travelers are familiar. It is cheap, considering that it condenses the United Kingdom and all the Continent of Europe, giving a large map, and nine others, with plans of 20 of the principal cities, and 120 engravings, for a guinea."—*Anglo-American Times.*

APPLETONS' RAILWAY GUIDE.—Containing Maps of the Principal Railways in the United States and the Canadas, and a General Map.

APPLETONS' NORTHERN and EASTERN GUIDE-BOOK.—Containing an account of the Principal Watering-Places and Summer Resorts in the New England and Middle States. A New Edition with revisions to date. $2.00

APPLETONS' WESTERN GUIDE-BOOK.—Containing all through Routes to the West and all Land Routes. The completest work of the kind published. (*Will be published early in May.*)

SKELETON ROUTES through England, Scotland, Ireland, Wales, Denmark, Norway, Sweden, Russia, Poland and Spain; with various ways of getting from place to place, the time occupied, and the cost of each journey for a party of four, with some of the principal things to see. 12mo. $1.00

NEW YORK ILLUSTRATED.—With 48 Illustrations and a Map, from drawings made by the best artists. The most complete illustrated memento of New York ever published. 8vo. Price, 50 cents; cloth, $1.00

Either of the above sent *post paid, by mail*, to any address, on receipt of the price. D. APPLETON & CO., Publishers, New York.

BOOKS PUBLISHED BY

J. S. REDFIELD,

140 Fulton Street, New York.

I. MODERN WOMEN AND WHAT IS SAID OF THEM. A Reprint of a Series of Articles in *The Saturday Review*, with an Introduction by Mrs. Lucia Gilbert Calhoun. *First Series.*
In one Volume, 12mo, handsomely printed and bound in cloth, beveled $2.00

II. MODERN WOMEN AND WHAT IS SAID OF THEM A Series of Articles Reprinted from *The Saturday Review*. *Second Series*
In one Volume, 12mo, 400 pp. Uniform with First Series. $2.00

III. TRIBUNE ESSAYS. Leading Articles contributed to *The New York Tribune*, from 1857 to 1863. By Charles T. Congdon, with an Introduction by Horace Greeley. In one Volume, 12mo, 400 pp. Extra Cloth. $1.50

IV HAND-BOOK OF PROGRESSIVE PHILOSOPHY. By Edward Schiller. One Volume, 12mo, Extra Cloth. $1.50

WALT WHITMAN'S BOOKS:

V. LEAVES OF GRASS. A new Edition, with additions and revisions. One Volume, 12mo, paper, uncut. $2.50

VI. PASSAGE TO INDIA. A Sequel to "Leaves of Grass." One Volume, 12mo, paper, uncut. $1.00

VII. DEMOCRATIC VISTAS (Prose). One Volume, 12mo, paper. .75

VIII. CONJUGAL SINS AGAINST THE LAWS OF LIFE AND HEALTH, and their Effects upon the Father, Mother and Child. By A. K. Gardner, A. M., M. D.
In one Volume, 12mo. Paper cover, $1.00; bound, $1.50

IX. ON THE USES OF WINES IN HEALTH AND DISEASE. By Francis E. Anstie, M. D., F. R. C. P. Paper. .50

X. MODERN PALMISTRY; OR THE BOOK OF THE HAND. Chiefly according to the systems of D'Arpentigny and Desbarrolles, with some account of the Gipsies. By A. R. Craig, M. A., with Illustrations. Extra Cloth. $1.75

XI. THE KIDNEY AND ITS DISEASES. By Dr. E. H. Dickson. Paper. .25

XII. REDFIELD'S HALF-DIME, VEST POCKET CITY MAPS. New York, now ready.

XIII. LITTLE BREECHES, by John Hay, illustrated by J. F. Engel. Beautifully done and printed by Photo-Lithography. .25

WORKS ON PHRENOLOGY.

NEW PHYSIOGNOMY; or Signs of Character, as manifested through Temperament and External Forms, and especially in the "Human Face Divine." 1000 Illustrations. By S. R. WELLS. Prices, $5, $8 and $10.

HOW TO READ CHARACTER. A new Illustrated Hand-Book of Phrenology and Physiognomy, for Students and Examiners, with a Chart for the Delineation of Character. 170 Engravings. Latest and best. For Practical Phrenologist. Paper. $1. Muslin, $1.25.

EDUCATION AND SELF IMPROVEMENT COMPLETE. Physiology—Animal and Mental; Self-Culture; Memory and Intellectual Improvement. One volume, $4.

LECTURES ON PHRENOLOGY. By GEO. COMBE. Pnrenological Mode of Investigation. One volume, 12mo. $1.75.

CONSTITUTION OF MAN. Considered in Relation to External Objects Revised. By GEO. COMBE. 20 Engravings and Portrait of Author. $1.75

MORAL PHILOSOPHY. By GEO. COMBE. Or, the Duties of Man considered in his Individual, Domestic and Social Capacities. Latest Revised edition, $1.75.

MENTAL SCIENCE. According to the Philosophy of Phrenology. Lectures by G. S. WEAVER. $1.50.

ANNUALS OF PHRENOLOGY AND PHYSIOGNOMY for 1865, '66, '67, '68, '69, '70, '71. Containing 400 pages, many portraits and biographies, with "How to Study Phrenology." The seven bound in one. $1.50.

PHRENOLOGY Proved, Illustrated and Applied. First principles. Illustrated. $1.75.

PHRENOLOGICAL BUSTS. Classification and Location of the Organs of the Brain, fully developed. Designed for Learners. Two sizes, the largest in box, $2. The smaller, at $1. (Sent by express.)

EDUCATION; Its elementary Principles founded on the Nature of Man. By SPURZHEIM. Excellent. $1.50.

DEFENCE OF PHRENOLOGY, $1.50. Natural Laws, Man, 75cts. Self-Instructor, 75cts. Phrenology and the Scripture, 25cts. Chart of Physiognomy, 25cts.

HOW TO WRITE—HOW TO TALK—HOW TO BEHAVE—HOW TO DO BUSINESS. Bound in one large handsome volume, post paid, $2.25. It is a capital Book for Agents.

Sent by mail, post-paid, on receipt of price, by S. R. WELLS, Publisher, 389 Broadway. Agents wanted.

N. B.—For sale by A. L. BANCROFT & CO., San Francisco, California.

STANDARD SCHOOL BOOKS
PUBLISHED AND
For sale by Charles Desilver,
No. 1229 Chestnut Street, Philadelphia.
And by Booksellers generally throughout the Union and the Canadas.

Descriptive Catalogues furnished on application, and any book sent by mail postage paid, on receipt of the advertised price.

STANDARD SPEAKERS.

Sargent's Standard Speaker, half roan, - - - - - -	$2 50
Sargent's Intermediate Standard Speaker, half-turkey morocco, - -	2 00
Sargent's Primary Standard Speaker, half-roan, - - - -	60
Sargent's Selections in Poetry, half-morocco, - - - - -	1 50
Frost's American Speaker, half-roan, - - - - - -	1 68

STANDARD SCHOOL HISTORIES.

Lord's History of the United States, half-morocco, - - - -	1 68
Lord's Modern History, half-morocco, - - - - - -	2 25
Summary of History, designed to accompany Lord's Modern History. 1 vol., 12mo., cloth, - - - - - - - - -	60
Frost's History of the United States. 12mo., half roan, - -	1 68
Frost's History of the United States, royal 18mo, half-roan, - -	1 00
History of England, Pinnock's improved edition of Goldsmith, revised by W. C. Taylor, LL. D., 1 vol. 12mo., half roan, - - - -	1 75
History of France, by W. C. Taylor, LL. D., 1 vol. 12mo., half-roan, -	1 75
History of Rome, Pinnock's improved edition of Goldsmith, revised by W. C. Taylor, LL. D., 1 vol. 12mo., half-roan, - - - -	1 75

NATURAL SCIENCES.

Johnston's Turner's Chemistry, half turkey, - - - - -	2 50
Johnston's Turner's Elements of Chemistry, 1 vol. 12mo., half-morocco,	1 68
Johnston's Natural Philosophy, 1 vol. 12mo., half-turkey morocco,	1 75
Johnston's Primary Natural Philosophy, 1 vol. 18mo., half-roan, -	75
Guy's Astronomy and Keith on the Globes, 1 vol. 12mo., half-roan,	1 25

CLASSICAL WORKS.

Virgil, Cæsar, Horace, Cicero, Sallust, Ovid, Juvenal, half-turkey morocco, each, - - - - - - - - - -	2 25
Xenophon's Anabasis, and Homer's Iliad, half-turkey morocco, each,	2 75
Clarke's Practical and Progressive Latin Grammar, half-turkey morocco,	1 75
Gospel of St. John, translation with the original Greek text, -	2 75
Livy. Interlinear translation by Hamilton and Clarke. (*In Press.*)	

To be followed by School Editions of other Classic Authors on the same plan.

For sale by A. L. Bancroft & Co,,
721 Market St., San Francisco, Cal.

KAY & BROTHER,

Law Publishers, Booksellers

AND IMPORTERS,

17 & 19 SOUTH SIXTH STREET,

PHILADELPHIA.

PUBLISH

Brightly's Digest of the Laws of the United States, 2 vols. 8vo.	$16.50
Brightly's Digest of Federal Decisions, 2 vols. 8vo.	13.50
Brightly's Bankrupt Law, 8vo.	3.00
Wharton's American Criminal Law, 3 vols. 8vo.	22.50
Wharton's Precedents of Indictments and Pleas, 2 vols. 8vo.	15.00
Wharton's Law Dictionary, 8vo.	7.50
Wharton's Conflict of Laws, or Private International Law, 8vo. (In preparation.)	
Wharton and Stelle's Medical Jurisprudence, 8vo.	8.00
Hilliard on Injunctions, 8vo.	7.50
Hilliard on New Trials, 8vo.	7.50
Hilliard on Contracts, 2 vols. 8vo. (In preparation.)	
Pennsylvania State Reports, vols, 13 to 63; 51 vols, 8vo. per vol.	4.50

etc., etc., etc., etc.

KAY & BROTHER always keep on hand a full assortment of the Current Law Publications, together with many books now either scarce or out of print, at the very lowest prices.

Letters of inquiry promptly answered.

BIG TREES,

Calaveras County, California,

First-Class Hotel Accommodations,

SPERRY & PERRY, Proprietors.

The Calaveras Group is the one known to the World as the Big Trees of California, and the one chiefly visited by tourists. It comprises the Mammoth and the South Park groves. The Mammoth grove contains ninety-three of these

Giants of the Forest,

among which are the

MOTHER OF THE FOREST, the bark from which was exhibited in the Crystal Palace, London; the

FATHER OF THE FOREST, through whose prostrate trunk thousands have ridden on horseback; and the

ORIGINAL BIG TREE, the stump of which forms the floor of the famous Pavilion, thirty-two feet in diameter.

The South Park grove, six miles distant, has thirteen hundred and eighty of these trees, many of them of immense size. One, still standing and growing, has the inner portion at the base burned out, making a room large enough to contain sixteen men on horseback at the same time; and yet, enough of the outer rim of the tree is left to support the colossal proportions above.

The Calaveras Group surpasses all others in the grandeur and beauty of its trees, and is the only one having hotel accommodations.

Tourists leaving Stockton will take the cars of the Copperopolis railroad at 9 o'clock, A. M., to Milton, twenty-eight miles, connecting with a daily line of Concord coaches via Winthrop's, for the Big Trees, making the entire distance in ten hours. At Murphy's, stages leave daily for Yosemite Valley per Hutching's new route, being the shortest and best to Yosemite Valley. A daily line of coaches leave Galt for the Big Trees. At Melton, and Murphy's, private conveyances can be obtained for the Big Trees and Yosemite Valley, at low rates.

THOMAS HOUSEWORTH, Agent,
317 and 319 *Montgomery St.*, San Francisco.

NEW HOTEL.

GILROY.

The Proprietors take pleasure in informing the public generally that they have opened the NEW HOTEL, the

HANNA HOUSE.

SITUATED IN THE

Business Centre of the City, near the R. R. Depot,

And fitted up in ELEGANT STYLE, and being thoroughly experienced in the business, can promise their patrons such attention and accommodations as are found in a

FIRST-CLASS HOUSE.

Everything about the House is entirely new, and of the best quality.

THE HOTEL COACH

Will be in constant attendance to convey passengers to and from the House FREE OF CHARGE.

The patronage of the public is respectfully solicited.

J. A. GORDON & CO.,
PROPRIETORS.

CITY

Livery and Sale Stables,

332 Bush Street,

Bet. *Montgomery and Kearny*,   *SAN FRANCISCO.*

M. MAGNER, - - Proprietor.

An entire new stock of fine young Horses, sound and free from vice, of fine style, and capable of going as fast as any gentleman cares to drive. Also new and elegant Wagons of all descriptions, which I will let to responsible parties at popular prices.

Saddle Horses for Ladies and Gentlemen,

Horses boarded with the very best of care, under my own supervision, at *prices to suit the times.* Patronage respectfully solicited.

M. MAGNER,
Formerly of the El Dorado Stables, Stockton.

Private Teams furnished for the Big Tree Grove and Yosemite Falls, to start from Stockton, or the terminus of the Visalia or Copperopolis Railroad.

GRAND HOTEL.

JOHNSON & CO., - - Proprietors.

SAN FRANCISCO, CALIFORNIA.

SAMUEL KELLETT,

MANUFACTURER OF

PLASTER

DECORATIONS,

No. 763

MARKET STREET,

San Francisco.

NEW YORK
Livery Stable.

CRITTENDEN & DALTON,

PROPRIETORS.

712 Mission Street, near Third,

Opposite Dr. Scudder's Church,   SAN FRANCISCO.

Four in Hand for Cliff House.

☛ Orders left at the Office of Grand Hotel promptly attended to.

TOURIST'S GUIDE ADVERTISER.

H. S. GREELEY, Manager,

Formerly of the Occidental, San Francisco.

Exchange Hotel,

San Jose.

First Street, corner St. Johns.

CENTRALLY LOCATED,

NEWLY FURNISHED.

Bath and Billiard Rooms, with Barber Shop attached.

Board, with Rooms, $2 a day,
OR $12.00 A WEEK.

Suites, $4 a day, or $20 a week.

THE NEW YOSEMITE HOTEL,

Fred. Leidig & Hugh Davanay,

PROPRIETORS.

This fine new Hotel is the first which the tourist reaches on entering the Valley, and is situated on the south bank of the Merced, in front of Cathedral Rock, about three miles from the entrance to the Valley. The main building is two stories in height, roomy, new and clean, plenty of pleasant, airy bedrooms. Table supplied with fresh mountain trout in abundance, in addition to fresh butter, milk, eggs, fruit and every other luxury of the mountains. A splendid stock of ice has been laid in for the comfort of summer visitors—a luxury not to be had elsewhere in the Valley. Bar well stocked with best qualities of Wines, Liquors and Cigars.

The famous Yosemite hostess, Mrs. Leidig, has charge of the domestic arrangements of the House, and the Proprietors, in person, give their whole attention to the accommodation of their guests.

OAKLAND !

TAYLOR'S
Carpet Store,

Cor. Broadway and Tenth Sts.,
OAKLAND, CAL.

CARPETS, Oil Cloth, Paper Hangings and Upholstery Goods. Body Brussels, Tapestry Brussels, Three Ply, Ingrain and Hemp Carpets.

OIL CLOTHS, all width and qualities.

PAPER HANGINGS, all styles and grades. Plain and Decorative Paper Hanging in all its branches.

A full and complete line of UPHOLSTERY GOODS always in stock.

Parties residing in Oakland and vicinity, and those contemplating removing to Oakland, will do well to call and examine our stock before purchasing elsewhere.

We Sell all Goods at San Francisco Prices !

CHAS. L. TAYLOR,
Cor. Broadway and Tenth Streets, Oakland.

Yosemite House.

STOCKTON, CAL.

ALEXANDER McBEAN, Prop'r.

NEW FIRST-CLASS HOTEL.

Main Street, bet. San Jose and Sutter.

Centrally Located, Finely Furnished.

BATH ROOMS, BARBER SHOP AND BILLIARD ROOM ATTACHED,

EXCELLENT TABLE, FINE ROOMS, GAS AND WATER THROUGHOUT.

Terms; $2.50 a day, $15.00 a week.

FREE COACH TO THE HOUSE.

LORING'S RAILWAY NOVELS!

WE COMMEND THEM TO ALL TRAVELERS.

ASK FOR THEM AT THE BOOKSTORES, AT THE DEPOT NEWS STANDS, OF THE BOYS IN THE CARS, AND ON THE BOATS.

LORING'S SUCCESSFUL BOOKS:

Louise M. Alcott's Moods,	$1.25
" " Three Proverb Stories,	.75
Virginia F. Townsend's Hollands,	1.25
" " The Mills of Tuxbury,	1.25
Laura Caxton's Marion Berkley,	1.50
George McDonald's Robert Falconer,	2.00
" " David Elginbrod,	1.75
" " Adele Cathcart,	1.75
" " Phantasies,	1.75
Mrs. A. D. T. Whitney's Hitherto,	2.00
" " " The Gayworthys,	2.00
" " " Patience Strong's Outings,	1.75
" " " Mother Goose for Grown Folks,	1.50
" " " Faith Gartney's Girlhood,	1.50

HENRY G. HANKS,
Assayer and Chemist,
AND DEALER IN
Fine Minerals, Fossils, Shells,
ETC., ETC., ETC.

Invites Tourists visiting San Francisco to call and examine his collection at

649 Clay Street,
(UP STAIRS.)

TEAMS AND SADDLE HORSES.

CHURCH & WALLACE,
386 First Street, San Jose.

Single Horse and Buggy to Almaden Mine,	$ 5 00
Elegant Double Teams,	10 00
Saddle Horses,	2 50

Teams ordered by Telegraph, will be on hand at the Railway Depot.

Woodward's Gardens, Mission St., bet. 13th and 14th, San Francisco, Cal.

THE CENTRAL PARK OF THE PACIFIC.
(See page 146.)

Yosemite and Big Tree Groves
VIA
Mariposa and Clark's or Coulterville.

Thus a person can leave Sacramento at noon, or San Francisco at 4 p. m. by the C P. R. R., remain over night at the junction of the Rail and Stage roads, the second night at White & Hatch's and arrive in the Valley of the Yosemite the next evening; or those who prefer can remain that night at Clark's and ride leisurely into the Valley early the next day. The latter course might be preferable to the majority of tourists, who would desire to visit en route the Mariposa Grove of Big Trees, which is but five miles from Clark's. The trail from Clark's leads through Alder Creek, Empire Camp, Sentinel Dome, Glacier Point, and the far-famed "Inspiration Point." From the latter is obtained the first grand view of this wonderful Valley, lying four thousand feet below the "Point."

LAKE TAHOE,
Via Stage fourteen miles from TRUCKEE

DONNER LAKE,
Three miles from either TRUCKEE or SUMMIT.

CALAVERAS BIG TREES,
Via Stage, sixty-five miles from GALT, or sixty-two miles from MOKELUMNE

THROUGH TICKETS:

C. P. R. R. OFFICE, 422 CALIFORNIA STREET.
    "   "   "   —   OAKLAND WHARF.
C. & N. W. Ry. "   445 CALIFORNIA STREET.
C. B. & M. R. R. "   214 MONTGOMERY STREET.
C. R. I. & P. R. R. "   208 MONTGOMERY STREET.
K. C. St. J. & C. B. R. R. OFFICE, 306 MONT. ST.

www.ingramcontent.com/pod-product-compliance
Lightning Source LLC
Chambersburg PA
CBHW030746250426
43672CB00028B/1099